A WORLD *of*
HORSES

A WORLD *of* HORSES

Jane Kidd
Consulting Editor

Howell Book House
New York

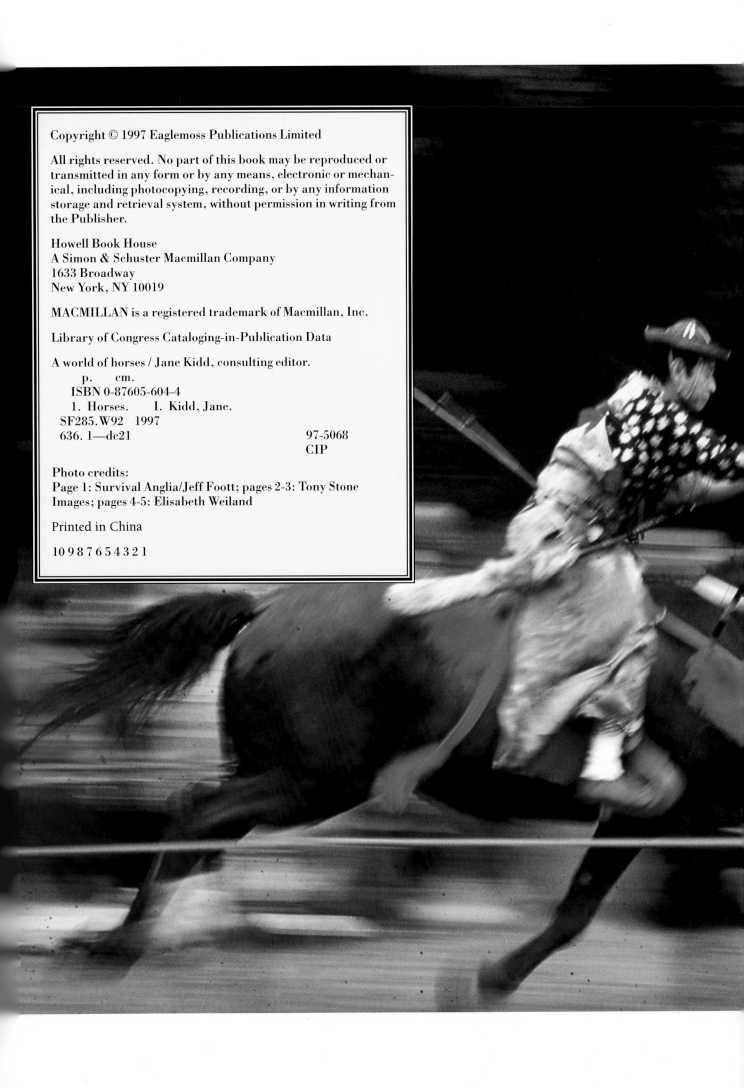

Howell Book House
A Simon & Schuster Macmillan Company
1633 Broadway
New York, NY 10019

MACMILLAN is a registered trademark of Macmillan, Inc.

Library of Congress Cataloging-in-Publication Data

A world of horses / Jane Kidd, consulting editor.
     p.   cm.
   ISBN 0-87605-604-4
   1. Horses.   I. Kidd, Jane.
 SF285.W92   1997
 636. 1—dc21   97-5068
                                      CIP

Photo credits:
Page 1: Survival Anglia/Jeff Foott; pages 2-3: Tony Stone Images; pages 4-5: Elisabeth Weiland

Printed in China

10 9 8 7 6 5 4 3 2 1

Contents

CHAPTER ONE
WORKING HORSES

Sleigh belles

Whatever the season, horses can be seen at work throughout the little villages and towns that nestle on the slopes of the Alps.

Sleigh rides in the snow

When winter comes in countries like Austria and Switzerland, horse-drawn sleighs are a familiar sight. At holiday resorts across the Alps, they carry visitors to their hotels and offer scenic rides along the mountain roads.

The sleigh-horses work hard – eight hours a day, with journeys up to 12 miles long – and wintry weather can make the going difficult. But, as night falls, they are sheltered in snug stalls beneath their owners' homes and are well fed to make sure that they stay fit and strong.

Summer pastures

When the snow melts, carts replace the sleighs. Instead of tourists, the horses pull loads of timber and farm produce – and sunny, summer pastures replace their winter lodgings.

In many regions, ponies are an essential part of the local life-style: tractors are no use on rocky mountain slopes and farmers rely on traditional horse power for all kinds of seasonal chores.

The sturdy Haflinger

Although many different types of horse and pony are used, the ideal Alpine breed is the Haflinger. Famous for its surefootedness and strength, the Haflinger has long been used for mountain work. It also makes an excellent riding pony – a quality which combines with

▼ ► During the winter months horse-drawn sleighs are a familiar tourist attraction in many Alpine resorts. At St Moritz, for example, visitors can enjoy the sight of horses bedecked with red plumes, tassles and jingling bells typical of Swiss-style harnesses.

the Haflinger's kindly nature to make it popular for trekking holidays.

With their chestnut coats and long blond manes and tails, the Haflingers are a delightful sight. For sleigh rides or special summer shows, they step out in brightly decorated harnesses – each region sporting its own style. In Switzerland, for example, red and white plumes and little bells are fashionable, while the Austrians favour richly decorated leather trappings.

Indeed, the Haflinger (named after the small Tyrolean town of Hafling) is much prized in its native Austria. All the ponies are carefully inspected to make sure they measure up to the high standards expected and Haflinger societies have been established around the world.

◄ **Haflingers**, with their chestnut coats and straw-coloured manes and tails, are the native ponies of Austria.

► **In Austria**, the traditional harnesses are made from beautifully worked leather and wood.

▼ **For winter work**, the Haflingers have specially adapted shoes. Two metal studs on the heel of each shoe dig into the snow providing extra grip on the icy slopes.

Pulling power

Brewery horses have been called 'gentle giants', and it is easy to understand why. In spite of their great size they are good natured, patient, calm and willing.

The horse-drawn dray

Breweries have found that the horse-drawn dray (the four-wheeled cart in which the barrels are transported) is the best way of delivering beer in towns.

The horses used by breweries are 'heavy horses'. They have such even temperaments that traffic doesn't fluster them, and their massive build means they can draw up to five tons each and 18½ tons as a pair. At Young's brewery in Wandsworth, London, 20 horses deliver 10,000 tons of beer each year!

As an added bonus the horses always attract attention, and so publicize the company name. The popularity of these horses was demonstrated when Courage opened their Shire Horse Centre to the public – in the first year it attracted 80,000 visitors.

At a show

For their everyday work in pulling the dray the horses wear special harnesses. For shows decorative features are added: heavily polished horse brasses, and brightly coloured ribbon or wool plaited into the mane.

At shows the horses are entered in singles, as pairs and as a four-horse team. They are matched for shows and so some colours are better than others – black is easy to match, while a lighter colour, such as grey, has many shades.

◄ **Pride and Prejudice,** a pair of Whitbread Brewery horses, wearing special ribbons, brasses and harnesses for a show.

▼ **Gentle giants** like the Shire horses below stand on average between 17-18 hands high and weigh up to a ton.

Every detail must be perfect because in teams they are judged as a unit: horses, drays and harnesses.

Threat of extinction

Among the more common heavy horse breeds are Shires, Clydesdales, Percherons and Suffolk Punches. Their great strength means they were once used widely as farm animals and draught horses.

When mechanization overtook traditional horse power, there was no need for such powerful animals and so many breeds of heavy horse seemed in danger of becoming extinct. However, heavy horses have recently undergone a revival and their most enthusiastic supporters are the breweries.

Care and training

Heavy horses used by breweries are well fed and cared for. They have to be in peak condition to pull the drays and to look their best at shows.

Two or three youngsters are bought every year. When they are about four years old they are ready for work – and are always teamed up with an experienced partner for their first outings.

Relaxing

One brewery (Whitbread) sends their horses for a holiday each summer to a hop farm in the rolling fields of the Kent countryside. Here they can kick up their heels and enjoy a well-earned break from the hustle and bustle of their working days in the city.

◄ ⅄ **Chosen to match:** Getting together such perfectly matched teams as these requires skill and experience. The horse buyer for a brewery has to decide how a foal's colouring might change as it grows up. Greys are particularly difficult as they can lighten by several shades.

► **Summer holidays:** Whitbread horses take an annual break at a hop farm in Kent. The oast-house in the far background is where the hops used to be dried.

▼ **A Shire mare and her foal.** Notice the white markings on the face and legs — a feature of all dark-coloured Shires. The foal also has 'feather', the silky hairs which grow on the legs of Shires.

English teamwork

At the turn of the century, farm horses were a familiar sight in the English countryside. Then, as machinery took over, it seemed they might disappear forever. But the farm horse has made a surprising comeback...

Horses or machinery

Today, many farms rely on machinery for doing large-scale work like ploughing and harvesting. But teams of horses are quite capable of such work. And unlike machines, a team can be split up and set to work singly.

Many day-to-day jobs can be done by one horse working alone: there's no point using a powerful tractor to move a few hay bales!

Special relationship

When people think of farm horses, one of the popular images is that of a ploughing team at work. It takes years to train a team, and a lifetime of experience to know how to tackle all the different soil conditions through the seasons.

Ploughmen use their voice to give commands but the words spoken differ from one county dialect to another. So if a horse changes owners, his first lesson is to learn the new vocabulary!

Care of the horse

The amount a farm horse eats depends on the type of work he does and the time of year. The average winter ration, for example, is about 5.5kg (12lb) of oats and 7.25kg (16lb) of meadow hay per day. The ration is adjusted to keep the horse fit but trim.

Brood mares work too. The exercise keeps them in good condition for breeding and they stay in the work team for as long as possible. Their foals are broken in at the age of two or three, but do not start work until they are four years old.

During the winter, farm horses are usually stabled, but in the summer they are turned out to grass at night. They also spend their retirement in a field.

Gentle giants

Although there are many different breeds of heavy horse, four in particular have always been popular in England.

The Shire is the most popular heavy horse. Although quite a slow worker, it is steady and strong and has a docile temperament. It is the largest of the breeds. The average weight of a working Shire is 940kg (2070lb).

The Clydesdale is the fastest and most agile of the heavy horses. It has a relatively slender build.

The Percheron is noted for its hard hooves, evolved to cope with the stone-block roads found in its native region in France.

The Suffolk Punch is known for its efficiency and courage in harness. It is a staunch horse with an ability to tolerate difficult working conditions.

➤ **Horses are more suited** than machinery to certain types of farm work as they adapt to all sorts of conditions. While machines can be hazardous in wet weather or on muddy slopes, horses persevere reliably with their work.

Putting on a single-cart harness

The horseman starts harnessing the farm horses after they have digested their breakfast. The procedure is:

☐ Put the collar on first, upside down because of its shape, and turn it round to sit on the horse's shoulders.

☐ Fit the hames into the grooves of the collar and fasten them at the base.

☐ Slip the bridle over the horse's head and do it up with a strap.

☐ Put on the saddle and secure it with a girth strap.

☐ Fix a crupper strap from saddle to tail.

☐ Attach a loin strap and quarter strap to the crupper. These keep the breeching strap in position round the horse's hindquarters.

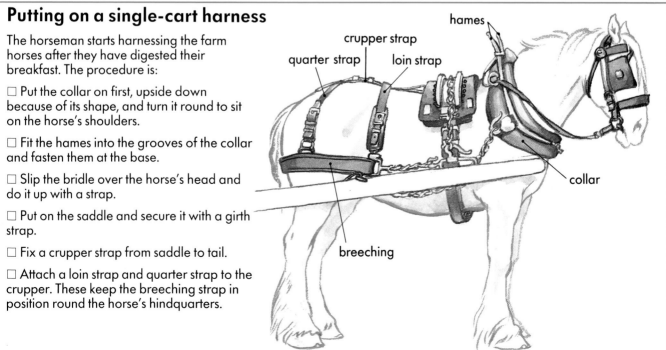

hames

crupper strap

quarter strap

loin strap

collar

breeching

17

◄ **At ploughing**
competitions teams
test their skill at
furrowing in a straight
line.

The horses are
turned out with
decorated harnesses,
brasses and bells.

These strawberry
roan Shires are
wearing ornamental
ear muffs.
Traditionally, the muffs
prevented flies from
irritating the horses'
ears in hot weather.

Now they are used
as decoration.

TRADITIONAL BRASSES

The brasses which
decorate the
harnesses of heavy
horses are like the
ancient charms used
to ward off bad luck.

The Crescent with a
star is a symbol of sun
and moon worship.

The Lincoln Imp is
from a county where
Shires were bred.

**The Three
Horseshoes** within a
larger shoe are
variations on the
earlier crescent shape.

The legend of the Gaucho

When the Spanish set out to conquer South America back in the 16th century, they took mounted soldiers with them and so introduced horses to the New World.

Roaming wild

In the fight for land that took place, many men lost their lives. Their horses – fine animals of Andalusian and Barb breeding – were left to wander alone on the open grassland (called 'pampas'). They had to fend for themselves in extreme weather conditions and only the hardiest survived.

Their descendants were called 'Criollos' (pronounced *Cree-o-yos*). They adapted to the dry pastures and, even today, many are the same dun colour that served as a natural camouflage in the pampas.

The bid for freedom

As the Spanish conquerors extended their control, some settlers objected to the strict colonial rule. They wanted to try living free on the plains.

These outcasts were called 'gauchos', which means 'born on the pampas'. Life was difficult for them and they soon realized that their survival depended on taming the wild horses. Only a horse could provide the gaucho with transport and a means of stealing cattle from the other settlers!

Taming the Criollo

Breaking in a wild Criollo was no easy task. First a man had to catch his horse by tricking it into a small, makeshift paddock.

He would then lasso the horse's front feet while a fellow gaucho helped to fit the bridle and saddle. A slip knot was made in the rope holding the horse's front legs. When the gaucho was mounted, a quick tug released the knot and rope.

The rider clung on while his wild➤

▲ **A gaucho's belt** was traditionally used for holding a knife and all the money he owned. Nowadays, wide belts decorated with silver coins are only worn for special occasions.

▼ **Today, gauchos** no longer live in the wide open plains of the pampas but work on ranches as ordinary farm hands.

➤ **Stirrups,** boots and spurs vary in style from one region to another. The ornate, crescent stirrup favoured by this gaucho, for example, shows that he comes from Argentina.

South
America

Uruguay
Argentina

▼ **The gaucho** was proud of his reputation for being able to ride long distances. He believed man's greatest goal was to ride a horse well.

The word 'gaucho' means 'born on the pampas' – but in Uruguay it also means a skilled horseman. In Argentina the name is less flattering: it is used to describe someone cunning!

horse bucked and kicked until it was exhausted and finally gave in. This method of breaking in horses – which meant life or death to the gaucho – is now the basis of rodeo spectaculars around the world.

The gaucho today

History has not been kind to the gauchos. When the open pampas was fenced and divided into farms, the gauchos lost their claim to the grasslands. Today, they have no land but their legend lives on – their proud way of life, their love of freedom and their skill with horses.

◄ **The relationship** between the gaucho and his horse is a close one and, together, they must be tough enough to deal with any kind of terrain.

► **Living off** the land as they did, the gauchos became skilled herdsmen and were the world's first cowboys.

Roll out the barrel

The decorated brewery horses at Munich's annual October festival attract a huge crowd of spectators.

Germany is a country famous for its beer, and to this day brewers use horse-drawn drays to deliver fresh supplies to their customers.

Adding colour

On special days, like the opening of a new inn, or celebrating an anniversary, the heavy draught horses and their continental waggons are colourfully decorated. Each appearance requires plenty of preparation to make sure everything looks its best.

How the trend began

The tradition of ornamenting the horses and their harnesses was started about 100 years ago by a brewer in Austria. Before long other Austrian brewers imitated him and the custom spread rapidly across to Germany, where today

Germany

Munich

▼ **Barrels** are stacked both above and below the dray: they are empty for these parades to make the load lighter for the horses.

the custom is still very popular.

The show harness is made of heavy leather and, if it includes a nameplate as its centrepiece, can cost thousands of pounds. Linen fastened to the inside of the collar harness prevents the rough leather from rubbing against the horse's neck and making it sore.

Training period

Horses can be taken on by a brewery when they are as young as two years old. Brewery horses have to learn to lean into their collars so they can haul their load. On their first lessons in a field near the stables they practise by pulling a log.

Then it is the responsibility of the drivers to get the youngsters used to the city traffic. These men in some cases have more than thirty years of experience in holding the reins and controlling the horses and drays.

The breeds used

The large company of Beck's Bier in Bremen has a stable with 11 Oldenburgs. These horses are raised on the lush green pastures of northern Germany and come from Arab stock.

Crossed with the heavy, cold-blooded breeds, the Oldenburgs are tall yet elegant horses. They stand up to 17.2 hands high and are the heaviest of the German warm-blooded breeds.

Originally, they were used as cavalry horses but, thanks to their well-muscled necks and shoulders, they have become good harness horses.

The Brabant (or Belgian Heavy Draught) is another popular breed with the breweries. It is one of the heaviest of the European draught horses and weighs up to 1090kg (171 stone)! Brabants have a docile temperament, willing nature and, when properly handled, are exceptionally strong workers.

Off duty

When not out on delivery work in the city or taking part in special events, the brewery horses are kept in stables out in the country.

Here they can get daily exercise, which is particularly important for horses of this size to ensure a healthy blood circulation.

A blacksmith keeps records of what shapes and sizes all the horses' feet are: every hoof is slightly different and requires an exactly fitting shoe so the horses can travel safely and comfortably over the hard road surfaces and cobblestones.

Brewery horses work until the age of 16 or 17. Then they retire from the brewery and have a well-earned rest out at grass in the country.

▼ **There are many** different breweries, and they take the opportunity to display their name and their horses at special parades.

▲ **At the summer fairs,** each horse is fitted with a shiny metal muzzle to stop it nipping anyone in the packed crowds.

▲ **The company** logo (emblem) hangs on a leather centrepiece at the front of this horse's collar.

▲ **Some drays** are decorated with hand-painted pictures.

► **Even** for everyday deliveries, the harness is livened up with details.

▼ **This emblem is** displayed on the breeching strap of the harness.

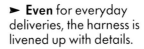

▲ **Rings** of flowers are placed round the barrels to add a dash of colour.

Pantomime ponies

◄ **Cinderella will** go to the ball! All the ponies in the troupe have French names. Little Pitou on the left is a Falabella, while Bijoux (meaning jewel) on the right is a miniature Shetland. Their owner, Russel Mack, is dressed as a Royal footman.

He puts their head plumes on at the last minute. The ponies can be mischievous, and shake their heads to toss the feathers off if they have to wear them too long.

There are some working horses who enjoy the glamour of the stage, and the troupe called Perriers Petite Ponies are literally groomed for stardom! They are the darlings of Cinderella pantomimes when they draw the fairytale coach that takes her to the ball.

Waiting in the wings

The ponies appear in ten performances per week in a 14-week run. There are two shows on most days – a matinée in the afternoon, and another performance in the evening.

Seven ponies make up the pantomime troupe, although only four ponies appear on stage – two pull Cinderella's carriage, and two more join them for the grand finale. Three extras act as 'understudies' in case they are needed.

Behind the scenes

The ponies' day begins at eight o'clock with a morning feed of sugar beet, corn and bran mix. Despite the long wait backstage before the ponies make their appearance, their pantomime schedule is not a heavy one, and they do not need large feeds. They are given a last feed of hay and sugar beet at night.

After breakfast, their owner, Russel Mack, walks the ponies through the town for half an hour to give them some fresh air and exercise. Then it's time to go backstage and prepare for the show.

Looking their best

All the ponies are groomed, and their feet and legs washed each day so they look their best. Grooming takes half an hour, and the ponies are tidied up again before they are called to go on stage.

Their outfits are specially made, and include elegant head-dresses and sparkling leg bands. Hoof oil is added as a final touch before they are led to the stage wings to be harnessed to the coach. They wait on cue to make their appearance, and are given a titbit to keep them happy. The hardest part is persuading them to stay still!

As they make their entrance, the orchestra strikes up the music, but the little ponies are trained to stay calm. When they come off stage they are given a tasty reward.

The 'stars' of the show make their last appearance at the finale, greeted by cheers from the audience.

▲ **The starlets** are stabled round the corner from the theatre. Their matching rugs were specially made for them.

► **A lift** takes the ponies down to backstage level. Although the ponies are sure footed, a ramp is placed over the theatre entrance steps so they don't trip.

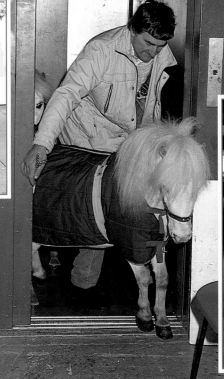

▼ **Like all stage stars,** it's important for the ponies to look their best. They are thoroughly groomed as they wait backstage before the show begins. Their coats are always kept clipped to look neat.

▼ **Glittering** leg bands add a touch of stage presence. The ponies do not wear shoes: metal ones would damage the stage, and rubber shoes make their feet sweat too much.

◄ **The troupe** can be quite a handful, and sometimes play up when it's time to put on their harness! They have a while to wait in the wings before they go on: the show is in three acts, but the troupe make its appearance more than half-way through, in the second act.

▼ **'Don't worry:** it'll be all right on the night . . .'

All the ponies get on well with one another. To try to keep the harmony, Russel chose only stallions. If he introduced a mare, there would of course be pandemonium — instead of a pantomime!

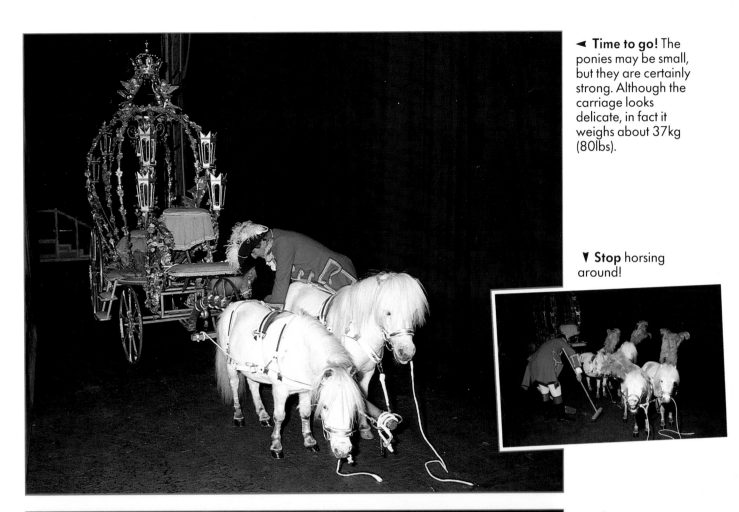

◄ **Time to go!** The ponies may be small, but they are certainly strong. Although the carriage looks delicate, in fact it weighs about 37kg (80lbs).

▼ **Stop** horsing around!

◄ **The ponies** make their entrance, quite unruffled by the music from the orchestra pit.

▼ **Cue** lights and special effects! The clouds are made of 'dry ice'. It is pumped on to the stage only seconds before it is needed as the haze soon disappears.

Logging in the forest

It's been many years since visitors to the New Forest last saw horses pulling timber out of the woods. But Peter and Sailor, two Clydesdales, have revived an ancient tradition. They and their owner, Bill Crowe, work on contract for the Forestry Commission, which looks after the 93,000 acres of forest and open land owned by the crown (i.e. the Queen).

Horses to the rescue

The forest includes stretches of woodland where trees are grown for industrial use. Heavy vehicles are normally used to drag the felled timber away but, after a long rainy spell, the tractors churned the soil into mud, and their wheels became firmly stuck.

Peter and Sailor were called in to help. Although they are heavy horses, their hooves do not disturb the soil and they can move easily through the trees. And, of course, the horses can walk to dense parts of the forest that a tractor can't reach.

The two Clydesdales used to pull drays for a brewery, and were accustomed to regular, heavy work. Horses that are worked steadily tend to be keener as well as fitter than horses who have been rested for long periods at grass. When Bill bought the pair, he knew that they would adapt readily to a variety of difficult tasks.

Training for new tasks

Although the horses are sturdy, Bill had to train them for their new assignment. Neither horse had ever worked in woods before, and they had to become familiar with their new surroundings. Pulling

▲ **The day** starts early for Bill and the horses – Peter, on the left, and Sailor. Even before they begin work, the horses walk the 21 km (13 miles) from stables to forest site – and at the end of the day, they walk back again!

► **The work** is heavy for both man and beast – and woman, too! Bill's assistant, Pauline, helps to line up the logs so that they can be fastened to chains.

Bill uses a two-wheel hitch cart which he designed and built with a friend. It has to be strong enough to take the dragging weight, but also be compact.

the heavy logs posed no problem because they were used to large loads. But at times, the horses would work singly, and they needed to learn routes through the forest.

Within a week or so they were used to their new routine, and knew exactly what to do. Bill didn't even have to give instructions to them! Peter and Sailor shuttled the logs between Bill and his assistant Pauline, who waited to receive the logs in another part of the clearing.

Once the team is under way, it can work up a good pace. On some days, the horses move up to ten tons in their eight-hour shift.

Not all the timber is sold to industry. Some is used by the Forestry Commission itself to make fences and 'dragon's teeth' obstacles to prevent motorists from parking on grass verges (the shoulders).

In demand

The horses are a popular workforce around the New Forest area where they live. In the winter, they do a delivery round, taking straw, hay and firewood to local farmers. They also help out on farms at other times of the year. In the spring and summer, the horses pull a spinner that is used for sowing seed and spreading fertilizer on fields.

The years of steady work have given Peter and Sailor a great deal of experience and made them safe and trustworthy. Once, the shaft of Sailor's cart snapped, and Bill was thrown off his seat to the ground. Sailor stopped immediately, making sure that his big hind hooves were well clear of Bill's head.

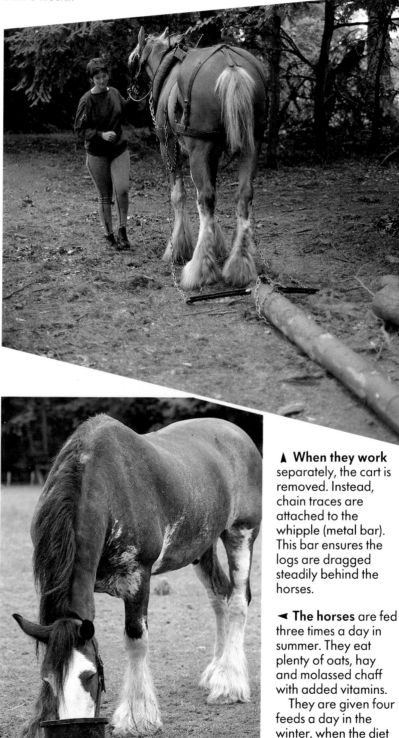

▲ **When they work** separately, the cart is removed. Instead, chain traces are attached to the whipple (metal bar). This bar ensures the logs are dragged steadily behind the horses.

◄ **The horses** are fed three times a day in summer. They eat plenty of oats, hay and molassed chaff with added vitamins.

They are given four feeds a day in the winter, when the diet is gradually changed to include rations of sugar beet and barley.

➤ **Ear muffs** help to keep the flies at bay. Comfort is all important for these hard-working horses. Peter and Sailor were measured carefully for their collars and bridles which were made to fit.

DIFFERENT CHARACTERS

The two horses have different personalities: Sailor, on the right, is the younger and faster of the two — sometimes he goes too fast, says Bill.

During breaks, Sailor can be guaranteed to find any titbits going begging, while Peter prefers to snatch a snooze.

Peter has a steadier temperament, though he lacks concentration at times, and without thinking heads down the wrong path in the woods when working alone! Then he has to be rescued.

▼ **Dickie Grayson** used to be a jockey before he became a stunt rider.

A day with film stars

There are only a handful of trainers who specialize in keeping horses for filming. It is a highly skilled career that requires a knowledge of horsemanship and film-making. Trainers with beautiful, well-schooled horses soon make a name for themselves and are much sought after by film and television companies.

Elementary, Watson!

Dave Goodey has worked with horses all his life, and keeps 80 horses, ponies and mules at his yard. They appear in many films and advertisements. One of the assignments was to supply racehorses for a series of Sherlock Holmes adventures being made for television.

▼ **The cameraman** films from a car that follows the horses as they race. Because the leading jockey's hat flew off half way through the first 'take', he had to throw it off at the same point each time they filmed it, so he looked the same in every shot.

▲ **Horses and jockeys** must be ready to start filming at a moment's notice. This horse plays the role of Silver Blaze.

▲ Between filming the horses are rugged up to keep them warm.

◄ **Dave Goodey** gives one of his riders last-minute advice. This was the first time she had been involved in filming.

The mystery centred on a kidnapped racehorse called Silver Blaze, named after his face marking. Blaze mysteriously disappeared, but Holmes tracked him down at a race meeting. The horse thieves disguised Silver Blaze by blacking his face with boot polish.

Hard work

Dave Goodey's horses were needed for several scenes in the episode. Even though the scenes would eventually last no more than ten minutes on the screen, filming them took three days.

Bangor, a small racecourse in north Wales, was chosen for the location. The horses had to travel up there the night before filming began, to settle in and be ready for an early start.

Unfortunately, the weather was rather miserable, and both horses and actors had to put up with bouts of heavy rain. Although a day's filming may sound glamorous, the process can be slow, with much waiting around which highly bred horses do not appreciate!

Every detail must be perfect for filming – the setting, the actors, and the lighting and sound, and there are often long breaks for adjustments to be made.

►**This character** plays a Victorian carthorse. As he only appears briefly in one scene, he has plenty of time to relax in the comfort of his 'dressing room'!

▼ **Silver Blaze** is led into the winner's enclosure.
The sound man holds up the extended microphone to catch the noise of the crowd.

►**Although** the girls are soaked through from the rain, the horses' needs come first. It's back to a warm box after the day's filming.

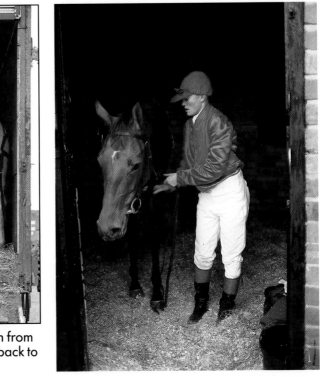

▲ **Shaving foam** is sprayed on the horse's neck to look as if he has been lathering. Actors in the background are in Victorian dress.

▲ **To follow** the actors as they walk along, a camera is strapped to the technician's chest. He walks backward as he films! The horses grow used to being surrounded by so many people.

◄ **Waiting** for his cue! The carthorse stands patiently while the cameras are set up for his scene.

▼ **Riding stunt man**, Greg Powell, gives a quick riding lesson to two actors. Placid and well-behaved horses are essential in this situation.

Bonnie Clydesdales

The horses belonging to the brewery firm of Carlton's are popular mascots throughout Australia. These magnificent Clydesdales are expertly looked after by a small team of grooms – among them Therese Devinish. For her, life never has a dull moment.

Busy schedule

Clydesdales have been delivering Carlton's beer for nearly a century now. Although much of the workforce has been replaced by trucks, the team of horses is kept up to preserve the brewery's proud traditions.

The big horses are stabled at the permanent showground close to Sydney's Centennial Park. It is a large park and as the Clydesdales need plenty of exercise it is the perfect place for early morning hacks and schooling sessions.

Although the Clydesdales are based in Sydney, they also travel throughout Australia to attend festivals, horse shows and parades. They make over 100 appearances a year. The Clydesdales have even been featured in their own television commercials and starred in an Australian movie.

A loyal groom

Therese is a great fan of the Carlton Clydesdales because they are so gentle and well behaved. She was determined to get a job grooming them – she even waited a year for a vacancy to turn up at the brewery.

Working life is varied for Therese. Sometimes she is away for weeks at a time as the horses travel round the ►

▼ **The Carlton Clydesdales** are a popular attraction at agricultural shows and festivals.

It takes up to six hours to prepare the Clydesdales for an appearance. They are carefully washed and groomed and their special harness is polished until it sparkles.

◄**Guinness,** a pet goat, lives with the Clydesdales at their stables in Sydney. He is very friendly and visits each of the horses to keep them company.

◄**Therese often takes** the Clydesdales out to graze in Sydney's Centennial Park. Here Oliver and Dave are more interested in nibbling each other than the grass.

◄**Therese sometimes** rides one Clydesdale and leads another on quiet early morning hacks through Sydney's Centennial Park. Here she exercises Mulga and Dave at the same time.

country. At home, they are given daily exercise and if the other grooms are busy, Therese has her work cut out and often has to take two horses out at a time. She rarely rides them faster than a trot because this is the pace the horses must keep to when working in a team of six.

Seaside trip

Botany Bay is near the stables, and every few weeks during the summer the grooms throw on their swimsuits and take the horses out swimming. The Clydesdales love it, as do the grooms, and swimming in the sea is excellent exercise. It gives the horses a really good workout, without straining their legs.

The grooms ride the horses into the water and let them stand quietly for a short time to cool down and get used to the new surroundings. It's important they stay calm, otherwise they could rush into the water too quickly, and accidentally hurt their riders by stepping on them with their enormous hooves.

Once they are relaxed, the grooms take the horses into deeper water. As they begin to swim, Therese and the other grooms paddle along while holding on to the horses' headcollars. Swimming regularly with the Clydesdales in the summer guarantees that the grooms are as fit as their horses and makes everyone return to work refreshed.

▼►**The Clydesdales** enjoy their sunny outings to Botany Bay. Even though the huge horses are natural swimmers, Therese talks to them constantly while they are in the water to reassure them.

Special delivery

The villagers of Cheadle Hulme, in the north of England, have their milk delivered in an unusual way – by a horse-pulled milk float. Each day at 6.30am sharp, Jim, a hard-working piebald gelding, is harnessed to his cart and begins his daily rounds through the streets of the village.

A family tradition

Jim is owned by the Leathers family and lives with them at Ladybridge Farm on the outskirts of the village. The Leathers have been delivering milk to the local community for over 100 years and it is a tradition that Mrs Leathers says the family intends to keep up.

A daily routine

Jim is nearly 20 years old and has worked with the Leathers for most of his life. At 6am he has a breakfast of pony nuts and carrots, and by 6.30 he is ready to set out on his 5km (3 mile) route. He is always accompanied by one of the Leathers – the whole family helps out on the round, including daughter Katie, who is always happy to lend a hand.

Jim has memorized the entire route through Cheadle Hulme – he knows

▲ **Jim pulls** a large brightly coloured cart around the village because his milk round is too big for a traditional two-wheeled milk float.

▶**David Leathers** and Jim are used to working as a team. When David stops at a house to deliver the milk, Jim carries on to the next house and waits for David to catch him up. Jim needs no driver as he knows the entire route by heart.

where to turn and exactly where to stop. There is no need for anyone to steer him. This leaves the Leathers free to deliver the milk to the front door of each house.

Jim is totally bomb-proof and takes no notice of the heavy traffic that travels through Cheadle Hulme each morning on its way to the neighbouring town of Stockport. Even the noisiest of lorries doesn't make him bat an eyelid.

Special treats

Jim's deliveries usually take him about three hours. He is very fit and does quite a bit of his route at a brisk trot. The only times he slows down are when friendly customers leave carrots out along the route for him. Mrs Leathers calls these breaks 'Jim's food stops' and says that he has grown to expect the treats every day!

Farm life

Once off duty, Jim is kept in his stable during the winter, and in the summer he relaxes out in a field.

Although he is a working horse, Jim is a great hit around Ladybridge Farm, especially with the local youngsters, who queue up for the chance of having a ride on him. Jim loves all the attention.

▲ **Mrs Sumners**, one of Jim's loyal customers, meets him every day on the route with a special treat. Some days she has carrots for him and other days it's hot buttered toast. Jim doesn't mind what it is — he loves his treats!

◄ **Jim has learned** to recognize the different traffic light signals. He waits patiently at a red light and moves off again when it turns green.

CHAPTER TWO

HORSES IN UNIFORM

All the Queen's horses . . .

The magnificent royal horses and coaches used for state occasions are a familiar sight to most people. The splendid spectacle they provide means a lot of hard work behind the scenes and the Queen employs a large team to care for her horses.

Choosing the horses

Thirty ceremonial horses are kept at the Queen's stables – the Royal Mews – in the grounds of Buckingham Palace. There are 10 greys (known as the Windsor Greys because they used to be kept at Windsor) and 20 bays. Each one is specially selected by the Crown Equerry and trained under the supervision of the Head Coachman.

▲ **The Royal Mews** were built in 1825 and house 30 horses. When no processions are being prepared, they are open to the public on Wednesday and Thursday throughout the year. Visitors can then see the carriages and the horses in their stables.

► **Built in 1910,** the Glass Coach is used for royal weddings. Here the coachman is wearing Full State livery, which includes a three-cornered (tricorne) hat decorated with ostrich feathers.

Opposite page, top: The 1902 State Landau is so called because it was specially made in 1902 for King Edward VII. It is painted a light maroon, decorated with gold leaf and upholstered in crimson satin.

The Crown Equerry looks for strong, well-tempered horses. They have to measure at least 16.2 hands high and be able to pull heavy carriages. The Queen chooses the horses' names herself and they often commemorate state visits. The two oldest Mews horses, Santiago and Rio, are named after the Queen's visit to Brazil and Chile 18 years ago.

Training

It takes up to four years of training before a horse is ready for ceremonial duties. As with police horses, the trainers use flags, drums, loud-speakers and a recording of the Queen's birthday parade to accustom the horses to the routine sounds of a ceremony.

► **A postilion rider,** wearing Ascot livery. This matches the Queen's racing colours – scarlet, very dark purple and gold.

◄ **Windsor Greys:** This pair is adorned with silver dressings which commemorate the Queen's Silver Jubilee. A complete set of state harness weighs 54kg (120lb) and takes two men to lift it on to the horse's back!

▼ **The Irish State Coach,** accompanied by postilions in Full State livery. The coach is a wet-weather alternative to the open carriages.

Their working life

The royal horses begin their working lives at the age of three. They may first live at Windsor or Hampton Court, before going to the Royal Mews, where they work in the indoor school or in the yard. A horse is not usually used for ceremonial work until the age of six when it is both strong and experienced.

Most of the horses now live in loose-boxes, although a few are still in stalls. Every horse is exercised for about one hour each day, usually outside.

The busiest time of year for the royal horse is during the summer. There's the Queen's birthday parade, visits by foreign heads of state, royal occasions such as weddings and, sometimes, the State Opening of Parliament.

The horses do manage to find time for a short autumn holiday, usually at Hampton Court. The horses work in winter, too – they draw the carriages when new ambassadors arrive in London.

Horses of the King's Troop

▼ **The six gun teams** of the King's Troop form up ready for inspection by the Commanding Officer. Each team is made up of six horses – the front pair sets the pace, the middle two are usually beginners and the back pair provides the breaking power. There are three riders to a team.

A 'detachment' of three horses and riders stands behind each cannon gun and the Number One (in charge of the team) stands at the front.

The King's Troop is the last surviving example in the world of a traditional horse artillery. The soldiers of the Troop keep their horses in tip-top condition at St John's Wood Barracks in London.

What the Troop does

The King's Troop is the saluting battery of Her Majesty's cavalry. Its responsibilities include firing salutes on royal occasions. It also provides a gun carriage and team of black horses for state and military funerals.

The Troop owes its name and existence to the Queen's father, George VI. In 1939 when most other horse artilleries had been mechanized, he requested that one should carry on the tradition.

The horses

There are about 120 King's Troop horses stabled at the barracks. They are of light cob stock – officially known as Light Irish Draught horses – and are brought over from Ireland at the age of four.

Their colour ranges from light bay through to bay, dark brown and black – but one rule is that they cannot be grey, piebald or skewbald. The adult horses are usually between 15.1 and 16.1 hands high, although some are as much as 18.2 hands high.

Training

When the horses first arrive in England, troop soldiers break them in at the army school of equitation in Melton Mowbray,

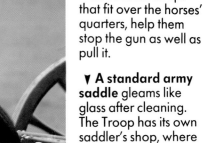

◄ **The two rear horses** – known as wheelers – are stockier and shorter than average. Their complicated harnesses, which include cross-straps that fit over the horses' quarters, help them stop the gun as well as pull it.

▼ **A standard army saddle** gleams like glass after cleaning. The Troop has its own saddler's shop, where the Master Saddler makes and repairs saddles.

Leicestershire. This takes 10 weeks.

Afterwards, the horses move to St John's Wood, where they are broken to harness and gradually introduced to parade work. The horses have to be both strong enough to pull the heavy artillery guns at a canter and agile enough to keep pace with the cavalry.

Life at the barracks

Only men are allowed to join the Troop and there are 170 soldiers and seven officers based at the barracks. Their lifestyle is disciplined and involves long hours of work. The soldiers spend most of their time training, exercising and looking after the horses, although they do learn modern military skills as well.

The horses are well cared for and live a busy life. Each horse is looked after by one man, and a close relationship soon develops between them.

To keep the horses at their best, life at the barracks revolves around a daily schedule. On Tuesdays and Thursdays the horses are ridden to Wormwood Scrubs Common. The rest of the week (except for their day off on Sunday) they are exercised from 6.30 to 8am on a scenic ride through the heart of London.

The Troop rides 'one to three' – each soldier exercises three horses at a time by riding one and leading one on either side.

Later on in the day the horses learn more sophisticated equestrian skills – including dressage and jumping. This is done in either the indoor or the outdoor riding school. The indoor one is furnished with mirrors, like a ballet ➤

★ **NAMES**
The officers' horses – known as chargers – are called names such as 'Dr Sebastian' after characters from the novels of a 19th-century writer.

The lines horses – who pull the guns – are given names that begin with the same letter as the surname of the Commanding Officer. The horse 'Oakleigh', for instance, was named after Major O'Grady. Each horse has his name displayed on a plaque in his stall.

► **As regular as clockwork** between 11am and midday the soldiers groom, feed and check over the horses to see they are healthy and free of injuries. This horse is being clipped before grooming.

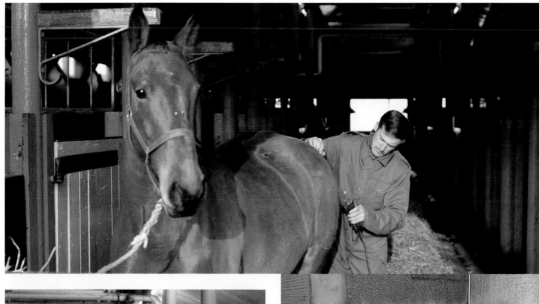

► **At the stables** each horse has a stall of his own, while the soldiers live four to a room at the barracks.

The forge at the barracks

As well as learning to ride well, some soldiers train as farriers. The barracks has its own fully equipped forge and, if a horse casts a shoe, it can be replaced immediately.

There are four trained farriers and three apprentices at the forge. Besides shoeing the horses every three to four weeks, they make special shoes to remedy any particular foot problems.

studio, making it easier to see and correct the horse's movements.

During exercise the horses wear a simple snaffle bit, but for parades they are tacked up with a port mouth reversible bit. This is a military bit, often used for driving, and gives more control.

Tack is always cleaned straight after use. Between 11am and midday the soldiers groom, feed and carefully check the horses. Each horse has a special diet according to his needs. The ingredients include horse and pony nuts, bran and oats. This is supplemented by chaff (chopped-up hay) and sugar beet to help digestion. On Saturday afternoons, the horses get a feed of bran mash because they are only walked out on Sundays.

Retirement from the Troop

Although they are superbly looked after, King's Troop horses live strenuous lives. At about the age of 16, they often start to show signs of old age. As soon as this happens, they retire. Some are bought by ex-army officers for saddle clubs associated with regiments, where they are used to teach children to ride.

▼ After hours of careful preparation, the King's Troop in all its finery is a magnificent sight.

Household Cavalry

▼ **Horses and troopers** must be prepared to do guard duty in all weathers. In winter, the troopers wear warm cloaks which cover their horses' hindquarters.

The Household Cavalry has an important and honoured role: to protect the Sovereign's life. On Royal ceremonial duties, a mounted guard rides ahead and behind the Royal carriage. If the Royal party were in danger, the guards could always provide protection.

On duty

Every year, tourists flock to London to see the guards perform another duty – the daily Changing of the Guard at Horse Guard's Parade. This is on the site of the headquarters of the British army in the Duke of Wellington's time.

The horses of the mounted guard are on duty for an hour at a time. They rest in stables behind the parade ground, but the main stables are at the nearby Knightsbridge barracks.

The guards' uniforms are in two sets of colours because the Household Cavalry is made up of two regiments. Troopers of the Blues and Royals Regiment wear dark blue tunics and red plumes in their helmets. The Life Guards wear red tunics and white plumed helmets.

Early start

At busy times, there may be up to 250 horses stabled at the barracks. A typical day begins at 6 o'clock in the morning. The men report to the stables, and consult a rota to see which horse they are in charge of, and what their duties are for the day.

The horses are mucked out and groomed, then tacked up ready for an hour's exercise. The Adjutant, (the officer in charge), inspects them before they go out. The horses on guard duty are exercised in the indoor school, while the others are taken out for roadwork.

Because there can be so many horses to exercise at once, the rides are split into small groups, and the troopers ride one horse and lead another. For safety, a single rider leads while another brings up the rear. The horses are fed when they get back.

Training the horses

The horses are black Irish heavy hunters. To be chosen for the Household Cavalry, a horse must be fully grown – about four years old – and in peak

▼ The Queen's Birthday Parade is a traditional ceremony. The Cavalry's trumpeters ride grey horses and form part of the Royal Standard party. The standard is a banner with the Royal coat of arms.

condition. A trooper in full uniform can weigh up to 100kg (16 stone) and the horse should carry this weight easily.

The young horse must also get used to the sword which forms part of the trooper's ceremonial dress. The sword hangs in a steel case fixed to the saddle. As the horse moves, it can bump against his flank and be wrongly interpreted as a leg aid.

Another unusual feature of the cavalry horse's life is guard duty: he must be trained to stand still patiently while hundreds of tourists pause to admire him and take his photograph!

Intensive course

Only men are recruited to the Household Cavalry, and they join between the ages of 16 and 25. They begin with basic army training. For some it may be the first time they have been on a horse, and they must learn to ride well in a short space of time. The troopers stay with the Cavalry for up to two years.

The regiments' farriers also take part in ceremonial duties. The farriers of the Blues and Royals have red plumes in their helmets, while those in the Life Guards have black plumes. They carry a ceremonial axe instead of a sword, which harks back to the time when farriers were responsible for dispatching badly injured horses after battle.

▲ **Rigorous inspections** take place every day, and the troopers score points if their horses are well-turned out and their uniforms in perfect order. Those who gain most points are chosen for mounted sentry duty; others are assigned for foot duty instead.

The neck chain was traditionally used for tying up the horse when the cavalry was out on a march.

► **The farriers** ride too. Their different coloured plumes and axes distinguish them from the rest of their regiment.

◄ **Other engagements** include the musical ride at shows such as the Royal Windsor. On such occasions they carry lances instead of swords. As they always hold the reins in one hand — directions are given by neck reining and leg aids — troopers need to be confident riders, fully in control of their horses.

▼ **With the all-important** duty of protecting their Sovereign, the Household Cavalry takes pride of place on Royal occasions. Here they head the carriage procession at Windsor for the Queen's 60th birthday.

The soldiers in the band of the Household Cavalry are excellent musicians as well as horsemen. The bandsmen need both hands to play the instruments, so they guide their horses using leg aids only. The reins are looped over their arms.

Chosen few

The band horses begin their career with the Household Cavalry, carrying out daily duties. The steadiest and most reliable are chosen to join the band horses only after they have proved themselves over several seasons.

Tradition dictates their colour and height. Trumpeters ride greys, while the drum horse must be coloured – skewbald, piebald or iron grey – and stand at least 17 hands high.

The drum horses are Clydesdales or Shires, strong enough to carry the weight of the heaviest ceremonial drums. These are made of silver, while the lighter drums used on less formal occasions are made of copper. When the horses are asked to remain still, they must learn to stand square to spread the heavy load. On parade, drum horses always walk at a dignified pace.

► **Preparation** just before an event takes time. The rider mounts, and then the drums are put in place one at a time.

▼ **A rare moment** off-duty at the Lord Mayor's Show. The red tassel is called a 'beard'. In days of battle, it acted as a deflector to protect the cavalry horse from an enemy blade.

▲ **Caractacus prepares to lead** the trumpeters for the celebrities' parade fanfare at the Horse of the Year Show. The ornamental covering over the drum horse's quarters is called a *shabraque*.

◄ **The State trumpet** also bears the Royal Coat of Arms embroidered on the trumpet banner.

▼ **Saluting the Queen** on her Birthday Parade. Eyes right, and drumsticks raised and crossed!

▼ **All Mounties' horses** are black. The colour was chosen because it best sets off the officers' uniforms!

The Canadian Mounties

According to legend, the Mountie – as any member of the Royal Canadian Mounted Police is known – is tall and brave. Astride his handsome horse, he fought off wolf-packs, and single-handedly tamed the Canadian West! The Mounties still have a place in Canada's police force, and the best horsemen also take part in displays staged all over the world.

Horses with a mission

The force to which the Mounties belong was founded in 1873, and its mission was to be in charge of the vast western plains known as the North-West Territories, and the Arctic North.

One policeman alone could be responsible for large areas of land and, in the early days, horses were the only means of transport. The Mounties then

◄ **The uniform** and equipment can be traced back to cavalry tradition. The saddle blankets are in the force's colours. The letters MP stand for Mounted Police.

▼ **The Musical Ride** is performed internationally – here seen at Windsor Castle. Thirty-two riders and horses are in the display.

The horses start to take part at the age of six, after rigorous training, and some star performers continue until they are 24 years old!

– as now – treated their horses with the greatest care and respect to get the best out of them.

All kinds of transport

Today's Mounties ride their horses when they act as escorts to important dignitaries, for parades and in displays. But Canada is the second largest country in the world – after China – and, to cover the vast territories of land and water, the police force now uses all kinds of modern transport.

Instead of sitting in a saddle, a Mountie takes to the seat of cars, trucks, aeroplanes and boats – and even snow-mobiles in winter – in his day-to-day patrol work.

The Musical Ride

Selected members – those who have undergone an intensive riding course – can take part in the Mounties' best-known display, the Musical Ride.

Its movements go back to early cavalry formations used during battle. Like other mounted troops throughout the world who also perform their own musical ride, the Mounties know the show requires precision-timing by both horses and riders. At each event, the accompanying band plays songs suitable for the occasion.

▲ **As added decoration,** a maple leaf, Canada's national emblem, is stencilled on each horse's rump.

► **The riders** must be able to work their horses individually as well as in troop formation.

The bamboo lances are 2.7m (9ft) long and have a steel, pointed end. When carried upright, the point rests in a support called a lance bucket which is strapped to the stirrup iron.

Home bred

The bloodline of a Mountie horse follows that of the Canadian Hunter – three-quarter to seven-eighths Thoroughbred. Most grow to between 15.3 and 17 hands. They are bred and raised at the Force's farm in Ontario. The huge 345-acre ranch includes stables, paddocks, indoor riding school and pastures. A staff of 77 is needed to keep the yard running smoothly!

The horses begin their training as three-year-olds. Obedience is emphasized throughout, because police horses must be well disciplined to stand to attention during long ceremonies.

◄ **The Mounties** swivel the lances as part of the display. The skill lies in staying in control of the horse with the reins in one hand, while handling the unwieldy lance with the other.

▼ **Charge!** This is the highlight of each performance, where the red-topped lances are lowered and the mounted divisions race toward each other at a full gallop.

The Mounties in winter

The Royal Canadian Mounted Police and their horses are important ambassadors for Canada, and they spend each summer travelling around the world, putting on their Musical Ride display. But winters are spent at home in the capital Ottawa.

▼ **The horses** can handle most weather conditions, and their coats are left to grow thick for the winter. Most of the horses get on well together — and as they are bred at the same stud, many are related!

Braving the cold

Their stables are just outside the city, where temperatures can fall to −20°C (−4°F), and although the snow can come up to the horses' bellies, they are quite happy to be out in the fields. The horses are let out for a few hours' exercise each day, providing there is no ice on the ground that they could slip and hurt themselves on. The Mounties say they prefer the younger mounts to let off steam outside as it keeps the horses happy and makes them easier to handle.

Eighty four horses are kept at the riding centre. All were bred at the same stud farm, which is several hours' drive away. There are 36 Mounties in the

troop, so each man is responsible for up to five horses. Five grooms help with grooming and mucking out, while the Mounties ensure the horses are exercised and in good health.

Routine exercise

Winter is a busy time at the Mounties' riding centre. It is the only time of year when all the horses are together. The day at the stables begins at 8am when the young horses are let out in the fields for exercise. Meanwhile, the older horses,▶

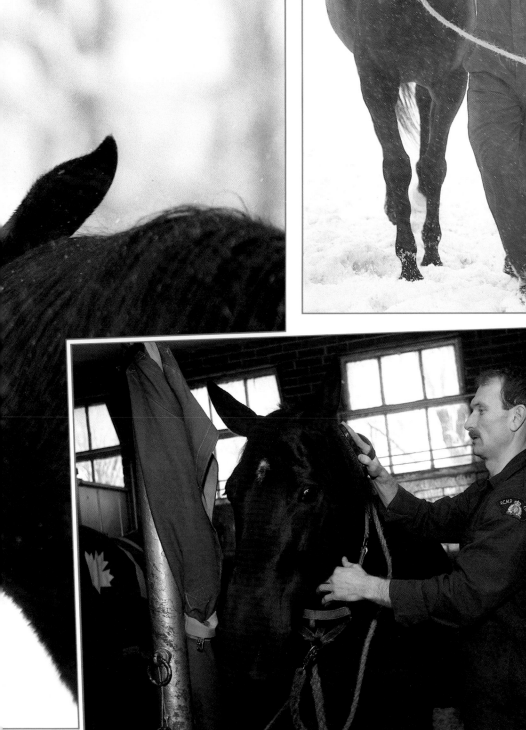

▲ **After their morning jaunt,** each horse is brought back to the stall individually. The riding centre has just five acres of land, so the horses' hay is grown at the big stud farm.

◀ **Each Mountie** is assigned a different set of horses every year, but inevitably, he has his favourites.

►**Although grooms** are employed to do the heavy stable work, the Mounties are responsible for their horses' tack. The same set is used both for practice and formal occasions, so it must always look spotless.

▼ **Winter practice** for the carriage horses used on formal occasions.

The corporal in the fur cap is one of the few women Mounties.

who take part in the Musical Ride, are fed, watered, and groomed, ready to begin the display practice in the covered school at 9am.

Before their riders mount them, the horses are led in a big circle to warm up, and they are cooled off in the same way after the practice an hour and a half later. By midday they have been groomed and are ready for their lunchtime feed.

Only 32 horses take part in the Musical Ride; the rest are used for other ceremonial duties, such as accompanying ministers and heads of state on official occasions. These horses are ridden in the covered school in the afternoon. They then return to their stalls to be groomed and fed.

The horses' day ends by 4.30pm. The valuable creatures are never left alone: the grooms work a system of night shifts so there is always someone at the stables to make sure the horses are safe and well.

◄**Youngsters** stay at the stud till they are three or four years old, and are gently introduced to a work schedule. The Mounties believe their horses should be fully grown before taking on official duties.

▼ **A different** Riding Instructor is put in charge of the Musical Ride each year, and he designs a new pattern of steps. There are always young horses and riders who have never taken part in a Musical Ride before, and it is up to him to make the display perfect in time for the summer season.

High-school French

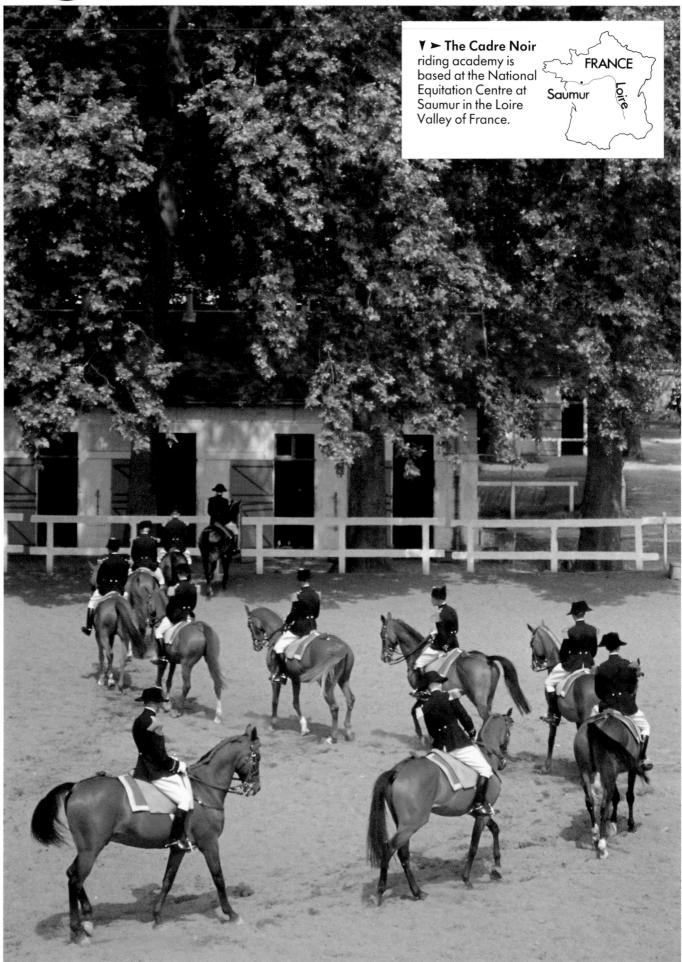

▼ ➤ **The Cadre Noir** riding academy is based at the National Equitation Centre at Saumur in the Loire Valley of France.

FRANCE

Saumur   Loire

The French Cadre Noir is famous throughout the horse world for its spectacular displays of advanced dressage. The dressage movements stretch the ability of both the horse and rider to the limits, and are the result of years of training.

Military links

The Cadre Noir was originally founded in 1593. Translated, the name means 'main military unit in black' – the colour of the traditional French cavalry uniform. The School has had a long association with the French Cavalry and its special dressage movements stem from the battlefield. At one time all members were from the army. Now only half the riders have a military background.

To become one of the 25 members of the Cadre Noir most riders are already successful dressage or jumping competitors. If their riding skills are not established, they have to pass a very difficult entrance examination.

The training

The riders teach the horses by 'asking' them to perform various movements at the flick of a whip. They use the whip to give signals and never as a punishment.

The horses follow the same training as any dressage horse and, at the age of six or seven, they begin special training to build up the correct muscles. It takes about three years to train a horse to perform sophisticated steps such as the flying changes of leg.

Dressage displays

The dressage displays, called reprises, are performed in two parts:

Reprise des Ecuyers: A brilliant ballet on horseback which includes all the classical dressage movements and is accompanied by music.

Reprise des Sauteurs en liberté means 'display of the free jump'. Some of the riders, and horses called Sauteurs (pronounced *so-ter*), are trained to perform athletic movements known as 'airs above the ground'. These steps were originally used in battle to help the cavalry out of difficult situations.

The riders of the Sauteurs have specially designed saddles. There are no stirrups, but a roll of padding at the back of the saddle and another roll at the front help to keep the riders in the correct position.

◄ ▼ All 25 member riders are highly skilled and give instruction at the riding centre.

The Cadre Noir members were originally given their special black uniforms to distinguish them from other army instructors who wore blue.

Today the Cadre Noir instructors who give riding lessons wear black uniforms and those who teach the theory of riding wear blue.

The traditional black pill box hat worn by all members is called a 'lampion'.

◄ **The Capriole** is the most difficult movement. It is the combination of two steps.

The first is the Courbette where the horse stands on his hindlegs, then jumps in the air and lands again just on his hindlegs.

This is followed almost immediately by the Croupade, where all four of the horse's legs are off the ground at the same time.

The horses are not shod on their hind feet for safety during their athletic jumps.

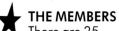 **VISITING THE CENTRE**

The Centre is open to the public from April until October each year when the Cadre Noir puts on performances for visitors two or three times each month.

The dates of the performances are decided each February.

DID YOU KNOW?

☐ The School has 450 horses.
☐ They eat 850 tons of food each year.
☐ They use 1,000 tons of straw for bedding.
☐ They produce 1,500 tons of manure.
☐ The blacksmiths require 18,000 horse-shoes every year.

★ **THE MEMBERS**
There are 25 member riders, headed by the chief rider who is traditionally known among his juniors as the 'Great God'.

Harmony and horsemanship

Lipizzaner stallions perform daily 'horse ballets' to classical music at the Spanish Riding School in Austria's capital – Vienna. The art of high-school riding has been strictly maintained here for 400 years and, each year, the horses travel around the world to share their magic with a wider audience.

The Spanish Riding School

It may seem confusing that the Spanish Riding School performs in Vienna. But the name is based on tradition; the school takes only Lipizzaner stallions – horses of Spanish origin. In all, they have 70 stallions but at least 25 of these may be abroad taking part in special 'travelling' shows.

The training

The trained movements are taught gradually and in stages, but the schooling is vigorous and demanding for both the horse and rider. Above all, the trainer must be patient and be familiar with the personality and temperament of each Lipizzaner.

The aim of the training is to make the horse so supple that he can easily change from a state of total concentration to one of complete relaxation. The exercises are based on natural movements but it needs hard work to make the horses equally responsive 'on demand'. Training begins when a stallion is three, and it takes another three years of intensive schooling before a horse is ready to participate in any of the formal displays.

Schools on the Ground

All the stallions must learn several basic movements (known as 'Schools on the Ground'). The steps include the *Piaffe* and the *Passage*. Another, the *Pirouette*, is made up of a demanding sequence of movements.

The Piaffe is a rhythmical trot on the spot. The horse's hooves come down in exactly the same place throughout, and he must not move forward.

The Passage (known in Vienna as the Spanish Step) requires the horse to rise off the ground and throw forward the diagonal pair of legs – so that he looks as if he is floating in the air.

The Pirouette involves cantering in a circle with the inner hindleg remaining in one spot.

Between the pillars

Another exercise is based on work between two pillars. These are round posts sunk into the ground at a distance of 1.5m (5ft) from each other.

Exercising between the pillars helps to strengthen the horse's muscles, especially his hindquarters, and limbers him up to make his joints as supple and flexible as possible.

Schools above the Ground

Although all the horses come from noble stock and have been specially bred to be strong and intelligent, there are more difficult movements that are only performed by some of the riders and horses. Not all are capable of perfecting the necessary skills, and those selected for training must be even more talented ➤

▲ **The sequences** are precise and difficult to achieve, but look effortless when they are performed.

◄ **The Lipizzaner** shows are still performed in the elegant riding hall built in Vienna, capital of Austria, in 1572. It is the only riding hall of its kind in the world. The sequence pictured here is the standard finale, called the Quadrille and performed by eight stallions.

and athletic than the other horses.

These special exercises are called 'Schools above the Ground' and, like all other displays at Vienna, are based on classical horsemanship. The movements require the horse to balance on his hindquarters with the forelegs lifted.

In the Pesade the horse raises his forelegs so that his body is at an angle of 45°. Less than this is a Levade.

The Courbette begins in the same way as a Pesade. The stallion must then take several jumps forward, but his forelegs must stay in the air and not touch the ground at any time.

Individual attention

As each stallion begins his schooling, the expert trainers give him individual attention. They can tell straight away

▼ **The horses** travel round the world to put on their displays, and attract attention wherever they go. Here they are being led through the city of Arles in France.

► **At the stadium** in Arles, the horses limber up before they begin practising for their performance.

how talented the horse is likely to be.

If a Lipizzaner looks suitable for Schools above the Ground, he has a different kind of training from the others. But all the stallions are assessed regularly and each is given the kind of exercises which suit him. The Spanish Riding School recognizes that a horse gives his best performance when he is relaxed and happy.

◄ **Horse and rider** form a bond of friendship as a result of working together so closely.

▼ **Each bridle** bears the crest of the Spanish Riding School.

▼ **Great concentration** is needed to perform the Courbette, as the Lipizzaner stallion has to balance himself perfectly. Long and careful training helps to achieve this difficult series of steps.

CHAPTER THREE
FESTIVAL HORSES

At driving shows in Cadiz, Spain, traditional handicraft decorates the harness. Just as in racing, each owner has his own harness colours.

Celebration time!

People love to celebrate, and all over the world they like to include their horses in the festivals. In some countries horses are at the very heart of the celebrations themselves.

The Japanese, for example, hold an event called Namaoi, which means 'wild horse chasing'. Once a year, horsemen dressed as Samurai warriors camp out overnight. In the morning, they make their way to a field to 'capture' wild horses and then release them. Centuries ago, this event was a religious occasion, and people believed catching the horses would strengthen them against their enemies.

Andalusia in southern Spain is another part of the world where people love their horses. El Rocio is a small town that lends its name to a big festival every Whitsun. Families from all over Spain arrive on horseback or travel in horse-drawn carriages to worship at a shrine. The beautiful horses of the region are taken through the streets, and riders dress in their best clothes for the occasion.

▼ **Tournaments** are held in Pirenopolis, central Brazil, every Whitsun. In between the mock battles, masked riders in bright disguises entertain the crowds and keep the carnival atmosphere going.

▶**Jerez,** in the heart of the Spanish sherry-making region, hosts a spectacular display of carriages known as a 'carousel'.

Among the popular attractions are the fine Andalusian horses belonging to the famous Domecq sherry company.

▼**At Whitsuntide,** many Spaniards ride to the town of El Rocio to visit the shrine. Their mounts are pure Andalusians or bay Iberians. Most are working cattle horses.

◄**May 1st** is a public holiday in France, and the Guardians of the Camargue celebrate with a feast day. The men own the famous Camargue horses, and gather for a special ceremony in the city of Arles.

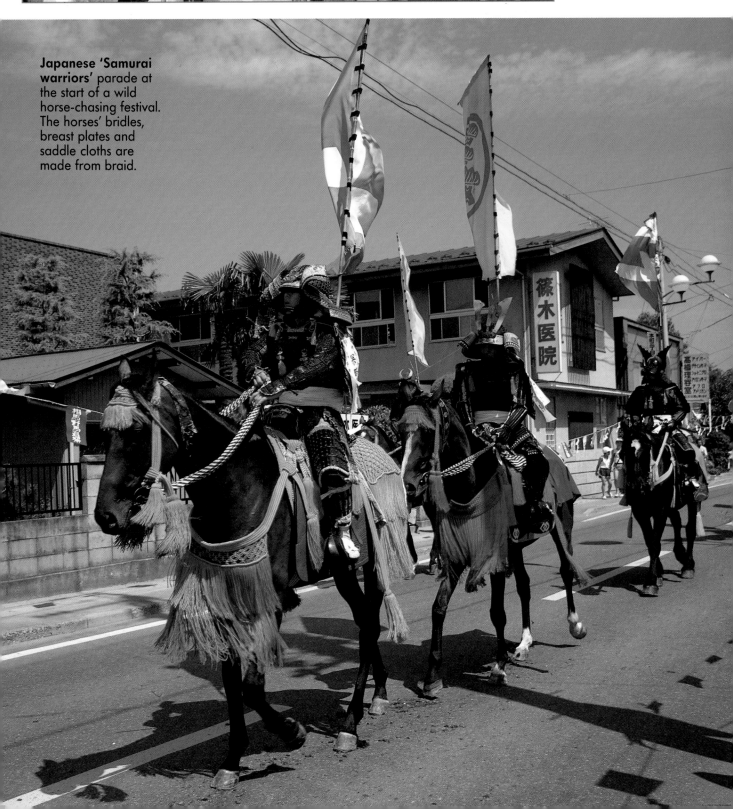

Japanese 'Samurai warriors' parade at the start of a wild horse-chasing festival. The horses' bridles, breast plates and saddle cloths are made from braid.

Masked riders of Sardinia

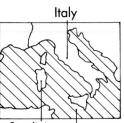

Italy

Sardinia
Mediterranean Sea

▲ **Sardinia**, an Italian island, lies in the middle of the Mediterranean Sea.

A MEETING OF NATIONS

This Sartiglia contest was performed at the America's Cup sailing competition in Australia. Jousters brought their horses over from Sardinia to Australia to ride them in the display.

► **In the jousting contest**, a star is suspended from a wire. The teams of horsemen have to thrust their swords through the star and knock it off the wire. This requires great skill and accurate riding.

⭐ **NATIVE HORSES**

Wild horses roam in the central mountainous area of Sardinia. Herds of horses are known to have lived in the region for thousands of years. But because they are timid, swift and intelligent creatures, they have rarely been caught from the wild, and no one knows how many of them there are.

They are known, however, to be small and red chestnut in colour.

The most important festival in the Sardinian city of Oristano is La Sartiglia, a jousting tournament on horseback.

How it all began

The origins of the contest date back to ancient games played by horsemen in the East, where a ring was suspended at the height of a man on horseback. Riders then competed to see who could catch the ring with a sword. The name 'La Sartiglia' comes from the Spanish word for 'a ring'.

Over time, a star has replaced the ring and the event in Sardinia has become part of the religious calendar. It is held each year on the last Sunday and Tuesday before Lent and signals the arrival of Spring.

The day begins with a herald who parades the city of Oristano on horseback inviting people to gather. Teams of horsemen travel from all over Sardinia to take part in the events.

The jousting contest begins at about two in the afternoon when the team captains and vice-captains assemble their men near the city's cathedral.

There is a Master of Ceremonies robed with a lace veil. When he mounts, the tournament begins.

Star turns

One by one the horsemen compete in a contest of skill. They gallop toward the star, which is hung from a stretch of wire, and pierce it first with their swords and then with a spear. To add to the drama, trumpets and tambourines play while the teams compete. If the jousting contestants are successful, it is said to mean good harvests that year.

Afterwards, the Master of Ceremonies reappears to bless everyone and the horses and riders stage a spectacular display.

The jousters now make way for the second event of the day: the horse race. The entrants represent their village or town, hoping to take home the winning prize – a pair of horses.

At the end of the day, everyone sits down to a big dinner which is followed by music, dancing and singing.

Sardinia and its horses

The island of Sardinia has been invaded by different conquerors throughout its history. The Spanish arrived in 1479 and, although their conquest ended in 1720, their influence on Sardinian costume and custom can still be seen.

There is no doubt that Andalusian horses came to Sardinia with their Spanish masters. The Sardinian horse of today is known for its slimness, grace and proud step and is likely to have descended from Andalusian crossbreeding.

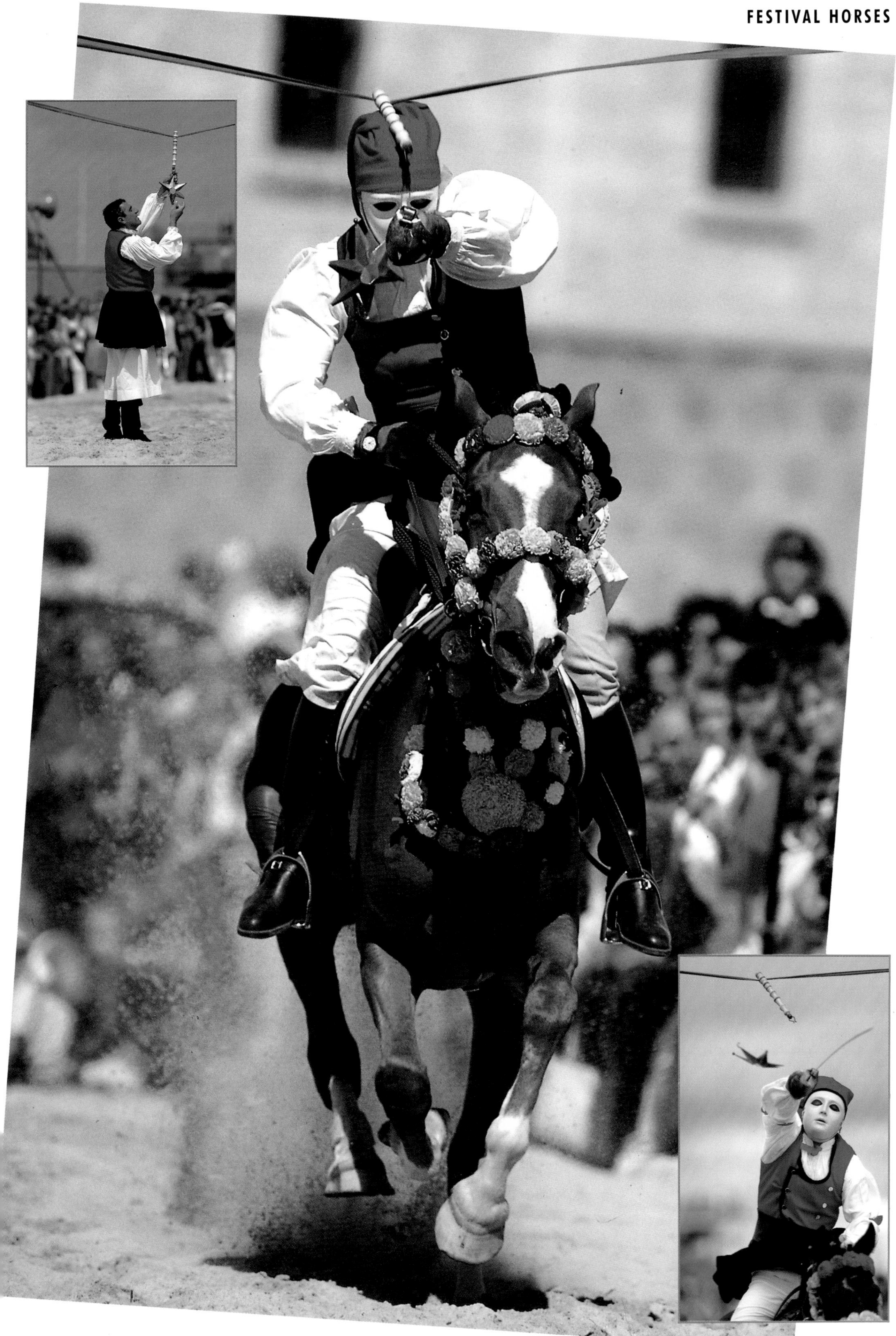

◄ **Once the Master of Ceremonies** is robed with his veil, he becomes a sacred figure and his feet must not touch the ground.

▼ **He is attended** by a horseman on either side.

➤ **After the tournament**, the riders put on a stunt display. Here one rider prepares to stand on the saddle and wave the Australian flag as the horses gallop past the spectators at the Festival of Sports.

◄ **Hand-made rosettes** of brightly coloured crêpe paper decorate the horses' bandaged tails as well as their manes, bridles and martingales.

▼ **The riders line up** to race each other after the jousting.

Afghanistan: highland games

There is an exciting horseback sport called *buzkashi* which is played in the uplands of Central Asia. The game originated centuries ago with the nomadic people of Mongolia, but today it is mostly associated with the tribal horsemen of Afghanistan.

How it is played

The word 'buzkashi' literally means 'goat dragging', although a stuffed calf skin is used in the game and serves as the 'ball'.

Two teams of riders chase the calf skin. The aim is to lift it up, sling it over the saddle and gallop away with it to score a goal. The opposing team must try to regain possession of the skin – so goals are hard to get, and cash prizes are given for each goal scored.

At the start of the buzkashi the calf skin is placed in the centre of a circle and the horsemen gather round it. The players wait for the rifle shot that announces the match has begun.

Goals are scored by heading off with the calf skin to a special turning point which can be up to three miles away.

Once there, the player rides a circle round the turning point, then gallops back to drop the calf skin in the centre of the circle where the game began.

When a rider thinks he has scored a goal, he lifts his whip high in the air, and the sponsor of the match must decide whether to award prize money.

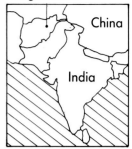

▲ **Afghanistan** is a barren region flanked by land on all sides.

◄ **The riders pictured** have a flying horse as their team emblem. Buzkashi horses are so prized that they are said to have wings when they are born: a foal should not touch the ground during birth – in case its wings are damaged!

▼ **Spectators** group themselves round their team flags. All the young men dream of becoming buzkashi riders and representing their village.

Tradition and change

Traditionally buzkashi was played on special holidays, but now anyone who has enough to offer as prize money can invite local horsemen to take part in a game.

Social upheaval in Afghanistan has forced many tribal horsemen to migrate to Pakistan, but they have taken their sport with them and the game is now played there.

Special training

Buzkashi is like a tougher version of polo. But the lack of firm rules makes it all the more wild and exhilarating. It can take five years to train a horse so it's good enough to take part. However excited, the horses must learn not to tread on a fallen rider, and to swerve away from collisions.

Great care is taken with the horses' breeding and day-to-day care. Buzkashi mounts must be agile, strong and fast.

It's not just the horses that have to be the best. Only the bravest and most skilful horsemen are chosen and, without set time limits or marked-out fields, the struggle for control produces fierce displays of fast and athletic riding.

▼ **As many as a** thousand riders have been known to take part in a single game of buzkashi.

▲ **Horses** are special to the Afghans and both they and their rugs (**inset**) indicate wealth.

▲ **The team emblem** on this rider's jacket shows he is from Jozjan province in the north. His hat is made from leather and wool.

▲ **The mountain ranges** of Afghanistan form a breathtaking backdrop to the buzkashi. Rival teams form separate groups as they gather for the match.

Sallah Day spectacular

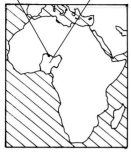

Katsina   Nigeria

▼ **For the festival** in Nigeria, west Africa, the horses are adorned with tassels and neckbands. Their riders wear robes studded with mirrors, semi-precious stones and gold thread.

Sallah Day is the most exciting day of the year for children and adults alike all over northern Nigeria.

Celebration time

Sallah Day ends the month-long Moslem fast of Ramadan, and is a time for feasting, parades and above all for the holding of a *durbar*, a spectacular display of daring horsemanship.

From early dawn, people from the surrounding countryside flock into the towns. Most of them walk, but some families arrive in little carts, pulled by one or two donkeys. These carts are normally used for bringing produce to market — vegetables, cotton or groundnuts ('peanuts'), for which the area is famous. The more prosperous farmers

and noblemen ride to the festival on the horses which later in the day will star in the durbar display.

Famous fortress

The most traditional — and the most impressive — Sallah Day ceremony is held in the ancient fortress of Katsina. The Emir (ruler) is one of the most powerful and influential men in the area.

On Sallah Day the city gates open to streams of colourfully dressed people. The large dusty square in front of the palace fills with people. They watch the Emir and his officials go past in a procession. An ancient ceremony then takes place: the Emir rides a circle round the outside of the city walls to

display to his people that he is still their ruler. The people also get the chance to put forward any requests and hand the Emir their petitions.

Gradually the procession moves to the main square, a huge area that on ordinary days is used for the city market. Today, the durbar is held here.

Teams prepare to gallop

The Emir dismounts to take his seat on a raised platform at one end of the square. At the other end hundreds of horsemen jostle for position and arrange themselves in lines of eight. Suddenly a fanfare sounds to announce that the durbar is about to begin.

At a signal, the first line or 'team' starts to gallop across the square▶

▲ **Jugglers and court musicians** lead the big procession to the city square where the riding display takes place.

▼ **Guards** protect the Emir (ruler) as he rides his white Arab stallion. Braid on the mane plaits and ornate embroidery add colour to the saddlery (inset).

toward the Emir. Halfway across the square each rider raises his gun with one hand and shoots into the air with a tremendous volley.

Now the riders urge their mounts on even faster toward the Emir's platform. Galloping at what seems an unstoppable pace, the horses are pulled up at the very last moment, their riders lifting their fists in salute to the Emir as they turn and ride away.

Skilled riders

In all the excitement of the competition, the riders seem in danger of falling off or crashing into the Emir's platform. Yet these are experts, with a long tradition of horsemanship behind them, their skills polished by daily practice. The riders stay firmly in their saddles.

As the last team hurtles across the square and slithers to a halt in a cloud of dust, the durbar is over.

But there is still one more ceremony before Sallah Day draws to a close: and this shows how respected the horse is in Nigeria. The Emir rides to the prayer ground where he dismounts. His horse is not led away, but stays close by the Emir as he takes his place in front of the crowds to lead them in prayer.

► **The Emir** is dressed all in white and covers his face with a light veil to save him breathing in the thick dust, kicked up by the hooves of hundreds of horses.

▼ **There is tremendous** rivalry between the teams of riders to see who can ride the fastest, fire the loudest shot, and who can ride nearest to their ruler as he watches the display.

The Feria of Seville

Spain

Seville

▼ **Seville** comes alive with colourful costumes and street decorations. Here horses and riders look for shade from the midday sun.

If you visited all the celebrations in Andalusia, southern Spain, it could take at least six months, as festival follows festival across the length of the area. They are called *ferias*, the Spanish word for cattle fairs, and this is what the holidays used to be.

Singing and dancing

One of the best-known and most lavish of these celebrations is the Feria of Seville. The original annual cattle and horse fair no longer takes place, but the horse is still the star attraction of the Feria today.

The festival starts about two weeks after Easter and goes on for six days and nights. It is a busy time for shops and restaurants, but everyone else has a holiday from work. People sing and dance to the sounds of guitars and castanets, and a huge funfair arrives, to the delight of the children.

Horses on parade

The highlight of each day is the parade of magnificent horses and ponies. Their bridles are decorated and their saddles covered with hand-embroidered quilts, in Moorish (north African) style.

The Andalusian women wear traditional flamenco (gypsy-like) frilly

dresses, and put roses in their hair. They ride pillion with their husbands, or on their own, or in a group behind their men. The men also take great pride in their clothes with their flat hats, short jackets and *zahonas* – their leather quilted aprons.

Children wear the same costumes as their parents. The boys hold the reins in one hand and keep the other hand placed on their waist. Some of the girls ride side-saddle.

Horses decorated with tassels and bobbles pull carriages that bring more children and babies. These too wear flamenco frills. The procession lasts from 11 o'clock in the morning till about five in the afternoon.

Temporary pavilions called *casetas* line the route. These are owned by clubs or groups of people and a prize is awarded for the most decorative one. These casetas provide their members with a viewpoint for the parade, and later in the evening members and their guests dance flamenco.

▼ **Children** also enjoy taking part. Note the unusual double bridle and leather fly fringe. The quilted pad attached to the back of the saddle, called a pillion, is for a lady companion.

◄ **Youngsters** wear traditional outfits too, though some girls prefer to dress like their brothers so they can ride astride! The silver box-like stirrups are typical of the region.

► **Andalusians** and Lusitanos are the main breeds of horse in Spain. The grey Andalusian has a typically long and flowing mane. Lusitanos are originally from Portugal. They are intelligent and athletic.

◄ **Mules** pull carriages that bring people to the festival. The harness is decorated with woven toggles to add a touch of colour.

◄ **Visitors** take rides round the city to see what is going on. This five-horse carriage is passing some of the many candy-striped pavilions where families sit and watch. When the sun sets, the street decorations will light up the evening's entertainment.

◄ **Processions** are popular in Fosses-La-Ville. Mounted 'soldiers' wear Napoleonic uniforms and carry flags. Care is taken to ensure the detail is historically correct.

The procession of St Feuillen

Marches are extremely popular in southern Belgium. The procession of St Feuillen (pronounced *Foy-in*) is one of the greatest attractions, drawing crowds of more than 50,000 people. The festival takes place in the pretty village of Fosses-La-Ville.

Saints and soldiers

There are two different characteristics of the procession. One is honouring the patron saint of the region, St Feuillen, an Irish monk who established a monastery in Fosses in the 17th century. The other is remembering the soldiers of battles fought in the area. This involves wearing splendid uniforms that create a festive and historic atmosphere. The most important influence is that of Napoleon.

In 1815, Napoleon gathered his troops together at L'Entre-Sambre-et-Meuse before the battle of Waterloo, and it is also from here that his great army retreated to France. The villagers picked up the uniforms left behind by his soldiers and tried to organize themselves into companies, mimicking the Napoleonic troops.

Since that time, some villagers have adopted uniforms to do with other battles. In today's procession, companies from many countries are well represented – including Algerian Zouaves, ➤

▲ **The village** of Fosses-La-Ville is in southern Belgium in an area known as L'Entre-Sambre-et-Meuse, meaning 'between the rivers Sambre and Meuse'.

THE CEREMONIES
The procession is held every seven years, on the last Sunday in September. The festivities begin the week before with a night mass.

Each morning a bugle is sounded, echoing the battle call, and, during the week, there are visits to the monuments of those killed in action, and a torchlight retreat with military musical accompaniment.

▲ **St Feuillen** arrived in Fosses-La-Ville in the year 650, and dedicated his life to missionary work.

◄ **Horses** are still used on farms in Belgium, and their work keeps them fit. They do not need extra training to take part in the re-enacted battle scenes.

▲ **One rider** dresses up as Napoleon. He wears the characteristic hat, and rides a white horse that resembles Marengo, the Emperor's Arab stallion.

➤ **Muskets** are fired, and the mock battle begins. The noise of the guns and the smell of gunpowder adds a realistic atmosphere.

▼ **The standard bearer's** job was to carry the flag of the regiment, in this case the cavalry of the Imperial Guard. An eagle emblem sits at the top of the pole.

Russian Hussars, English Grenadiers and even the Royal Canadian Mounted Police. But mostly the uniforms stand for Napoleon's empire.

The costumes belong to the villagers. Some of the very lucky ones may have an original uniform; others lovingly tailor their own.

Their horses

Horses play a considerable role in the march. All officers are mounted and the horses are turned out in the correct tack of the period.

Most people in the province are farmers and they use their working horses on the marches. The horses are very fit from the tasks they do on the farms every day, and they make sturdy and reliable mounts for the procession.

On the day

After months of preparation, more than 2,000 'soldiers' on horseback from Fosses and surrounding villages take part. Even small children have the chance to play a foot soldier in Napoleon's army.

By eight o'clock in the morning, the streets are filled with horses, officers, drummers, musicians and soldiers making their way to the market place for the 'Grand Tour'. The tour is about 12km

▲ Children dress up too in outfits made for the occasion. This boy finds battle too noisy.

▼ The standards were originally made of silk, colourfully embroidered. Medals of a bygone age are pinned to the bearer and to the standard for the festival.

(7½ miles) long. It starts in the village and follows a route round the surrounding countryside.

Marching orders

During the course of the march, three battalions 'square-off' in battle position at three points during the day. The third time, they re-enact a battle. The soldiers form a 'front line', 200m (220yd) wide, and charge together down a hill, beating drums and firing their guns. It's very life like, and spectators can see what a charge to battle must really be like first-hand.

While crossing the St Feuillen woods, the soldiers remember the other reason for the procession; the patron saint. The monk died at the hands of robbers in the woods and, in honour of his memory, the soldiers ride through the woods, firing their guns non-stop to scare off the ghosts of his attackers.

Closing ceremonies

The procession finally draws to a close and is completed with the tradition of 'feu-de-file'. Every soldier fires a blank cartridge in the churchyard in front of the statue of St Feuillen. This tribute marks the end of the week-long celebrations, until it all takes place again in another seven years.

The Golega fair in Portugal

Golega (pronounced *'Golga'*) is a sleepy Portuguese market town about 70 miles north east of Lisbon. Every year in mid-November, however, it becomes a lively centre that attracts horsemen from all over the country, and from abroad, when nearly 100 horses converge in Golega for the horse fair.

Horse traders

Golega is in a lush valley beside the River Tagus and has for centuries been a meeting point for traders in Portugal. There has been an annual horse fair there since 1972.

In Portugal, a horse has always been a symbol of wealth and the week-long fair in Golega is the place to buy and sell horses. Private deals are struck for the horses, but it is not till the last day of the fair, the Sunday, that the auction is held in the town centre. This way everyone can see all the horses on sale.

Twelve of the best stallions from Portugal's National Stud are also exhibited at the fair. The stud is based 20 miles away and was founded in 1887. There are over 80 stallions there, mostly fiery spirited Lusitanos. The free-moving Alter-Real is the next most prominent breed, and the stud also keeps Arabs and Thoroughbreds.

Proud displays

As well as trading, people go to the fair to see and be seen, and proud owners show off their beautiful horses in the town centre.

Coach-loads of people arrive in Golega throughout horse-fair week, and the daily parade continues late into the night. There are food stalls and open barbecues.

There is also a chance for everyone to dress in traditional costume, which is nowadays worn only on festival days. The riders' buckles are studded with silver, and they wear smart felt hats.

Portugal
Spain
Golega
River Tagus
Lisbon

▲ **As Golega** is by a river, it is a natural meeting point for traders and horse dealers.

◄ **Children** also parade on horseback, to show prospective buyers at the fair that their parents' horses are quiet to handle.

▼ **People gather** to watch the daily riding parades, and to decide which horses they might like to buy.

◄ **Driving horses** are also for sale at Golega fair. This horse is a Lusitano. The breed is most often grey in colour, but can also be bay. All Portuguese breeds are closely related to those of neighbouring Spain.

▼ **Young horses** are lunged to show off their paces.

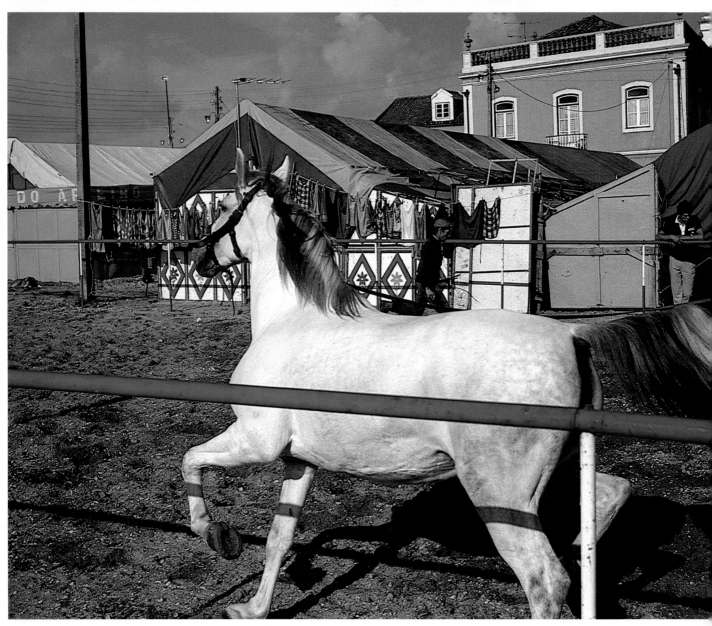

► **Riders** make every effort to ensure that they and their horses look their best at all times. Some horses have their manes plaited Arab-style. The stirrups are made of silver, and the riding style is a mixture of military and Western.

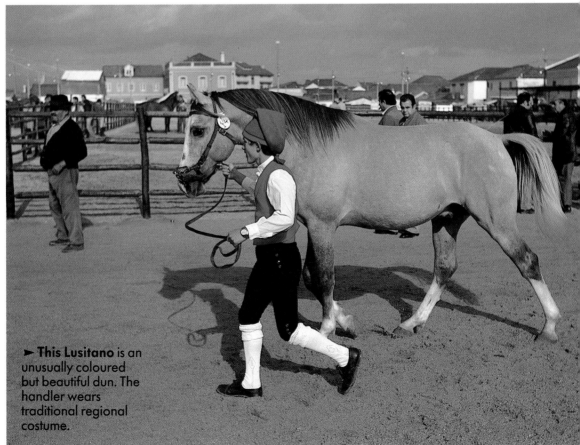

► **This Lusitano** is an unusually coloured but beautiful dun. The handler wears traditional regional costume.

Spearing the dragon

The *Drachenstich*, or 'Spearing of the dragon', is one of the oldest – and possibly the most spectacular – of all German folk festivals. It was first held more than 500 years ago.

An old fairy tale

The festival was originally held in honour of St George. There are many legends about this brave knight and most agree that he fought and killed a dragon to save the daughter of a king.

In the German version of the legend, the dragon was said to live in thick forests just outside a small town. One day, it emerged from its hideout, breathing fire and destroying all in its path. Townsfolk ran for their lives and were

◄ **Horses from local** riding schools take pride of place in street processions.
▼ **Furth im Wald** is a small, border town.

saved only when their princess offered to sacrifice herself to the dragon. Just as she was about to die, a local knight galloped to the rescue on his noble horse and slayed the monster.

Today, this story is re-enacted in the same town during the second week of every August. The town, Furth im Wald (or 'river crossing in the woods') lies on the border and, because foreign armies often invaded it, the dragon became a symbol of all evil forces.

Horse power

More than 200 horses take part in the week-long festival. In the past, local farmers rode their own animals but, because of tractors, few now keep any.

▼ ➤ **Locals dress up** in historical costume and re-live the day when a fiery dragon terrorized their town.

► **Horses who** take part in the dragon festival have dress rehearsals first – to make sure they are not frightened by all the noise and excitement on the day.

▼ **By the time** he faces the dragon, the knight is well prepared: his horse is trained for weeks in advance.

Men sit inside the dragon, operating the controls: a motor makes the beast flap its wings, breathe fire and spew blood before it dies!

Instead, local riding stables and breweries willingly provide the horse power. They know how popular the dragon festival is, and are proud if their horses are chosen to take part in the procession.

The horses are first put through their paces in early July. Every kind of breed is used, from sturdy Haflingers to heavy draught horses. The big breeds are needed to pull the colourful procession floats and no expense is spared in transporting them to the town. One year, there were not enough local horses and some were even brought in from neighbouring Czechoslovakia!

Star of the show is undoubtedly the horse which carries the knight. He must bear his rider into 'battle', through cheering, noisy crowds, and face a fire-breathing dragon without a sign of flinching.

Time to celebrate

Everyone in town gets a chance to dress up in historical clothing and join in the fun. A big procession files through the streets each day and local bands join the floats. The knight follows this carnival and fights the dragon only when the last parade is over.

As Sunday evening approaches, crowds make their way to the town centre to watch the knight slay the dragon. The nine-ton creature is a model built around a fork-lift truck! It even has a motor so it can 'fight back'.

Tension mounts as the battle begins. After making several unsuccessful passes, the brave knight stages a final charge toward the beast, throwing his spear into the dragon's mouth as he gallops by. People cheer, church bells ring and trumpets sound. The dragon is dead – at least for another year.

◄ **After playing** their part in the street procession, this pair can relax and enjoy a well-earned break from all the excitement.

▼ **Knight work** makes you thirsty! Fountains are the perfect way for horse and rider to cool off.

Austria   Hungary
River Tisza
Italy

The cowboys live and work on the eastern plains of the River Tisza in Hungary. They are careful to build up a bond of trust with their horses, essential for a good working relationship.

The men wear a flowing cotton outfit, felt hat and woollen waistcoat, for traditional displays, although their working clothes are more practical.

Hungarian high-steppers

It's tempting to think that North and South America are the only 'cowboy' continents in the world. But Hungary, with its vast, open plains and large ranches, has herdsmen whose riding skills are equal to any.

Mutual trust

Across the plains east of the River Tisza, Hungarian cowboys have long been a traditional part of farming life. As horsemen, they are the most respected cattleherders in the villages, and are proud of their working partnership with the horses.

The cowboys are known as *csikós* (pronounced as 'chi-kosh'), meaning 'horse-herder'. It comes from the Hungarian word for foal or colt, *csikó* (pronounced 'chico'). The cowboys were expected to work long days and travel great distances as they cared for scattered herds of cattle. During quiet moments, they practised their riding skills and competed with one another to see who could perform the most daring and demanding acrobatics.

The men built up an understanding with their horses, grounded on a mutual

▲ **The horse** listens to the crack of the whip for his rider's next instruction.

◄ **The Hungarian Half-Bred** is a popular working horse. As the name implies, it is of mixed descent, with a touch of Arab and Thoroughbred.

◄ **The horses** are trained to perform any movement their riders ask of them. They respond to the *sound* the thong makes as it is flourished in the air; whips are not used *on* the horses.

► **Harness-like** straps ensure the horses keep pace with one another. Even at top speed the riders are able to maintain their balance.

▼ **The cattle** seem to take the daring trick riding in their stride! Notice how the rider bends at the knees in rhythm with the horses' action. This is the secret of staying on.

trust. The key to their displays was a 'secret' language. Each cowboy carried a long, leather whip. By cracking it in the air, the cowboy 'spoke' to his horse and it could interpret the many different sounds. Great practice and skill was required on the part of the cowboy to get just the right sound. He had to master the whip 'language' perfectly before he could train his horse to respond to it.

Hungarian posts

The skills developed by the cowboys soon became a popular attraction, and special displays by them were always a feature of local festivals. Show pieces included making the horses rear up, leap through the air, and lie flat on the ground with the cowboys standing on their flanks.

Today, the best horsemen and their mounts are chosen to perform at shows around the world. The highlight of every performance is the Hungarian Post, a daring manoeuvre, which requires the cowboy to stand with one foot on the rump of each of two horses.

More complicated displays involve five horses: the rider balances on the rear two while steering the lead three horses as they run abreast.

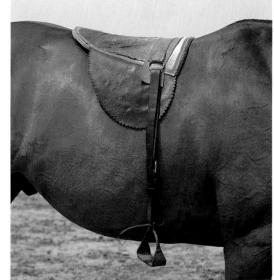

◄ **The saddles** in this cattle-herding region are unusual. There is no girth, and they are held in place by the rider's weight.

▲ **Each cowboy** has his own leather whip which originally served to steer the cattle. The whips have a wooden handle and a thong of braided leather, measuring some 10m (33ft) in length.

◄ **The Hungarian Post** is a great feat of balance and control. It is normally performed with up to five horses, but crowds at the Royal International Horse Show were treated to a spectacular six-horse display!

The art of Yabusame

Horsemanship and archery were of great importance to Japanese warriors, called the Samurai. In battle, their life depended on their horses and their shooting skills.

Bringing good luck

The ancient Japanese art of Yabusame (pronounced *yaboosamee*) means shoot-ing an arrow from a galloping horse. If a Samurai warrior did well in Yabusame, he saw it as an omen that he would defeat the enemy in his next battle. People would also examine hoofprints made by the horses after a display, and interpret them as omens for future harvests.

Today, Yabusame survives as a sport. Every November, Yabusame displays are held in Tokyo's Meiji Shinto Shrine. In the Japanese religion of Shinto, horses were dedicated to the gods, and even today, horses are kept near shrines to

▼ **Yabusame** is archery on horseback, a sport played by the Japanese. The targets are balanced on bamboo poles, closely watched by three judges.

bring the people good luck.

Yabusame horses and riders make their way to the archery course in a solemn procession. There can be up to 30 riders taking part. Helpers carry their weaponry for them. All are dressed in the colourful costumes of the 15th century Samurai, and the horses are adorned with tassels.

When the master of ceremony gives the starting signal, one rider after the other gallops along a marked course and has to shoot three arrows at the targets. The rider needs both hands to hold the large bow and arrow, so his horse must gallop without guidance down the course, which is staked out with ropes to help keep him straight.

Practice runs

Most of the 'warriors' work in offices and practise their riding and archery in their free time. They own the horses they ride, which are small and agile.

Yabusame horses are about the size of polo ponies and need similar qualities: the ability to put in quick bursts of speed, and to guide themselves while their rider focuses his whole attention on playing the sport.

► **The riders** must be able to balance and take perfect aim while astride their speeding horses.

▼ **The master of ceremony** is also on horseback. He mounts from the right side of the horse, although no-one is certain where this practice stems from. White is the symbol of purity in the Shinto religion, and so is a popular colour for a horse.

The Nations Cup

Any sporting event where teams from all over the world take part is called a Nations Cup. But perhaps the best-known competition of them all is the Nations Cup for show jumping.

▼ John Whitaker and Henderson Milton jump a double clear round at Hickstead in 1991 for a record-breaking third year running.

The first Cup

The first was held in June 1909 at the International Horse Show at Olympia. The King Edward VII Gold Cup, valued at £500, was made specially for the occasion. Teams of three army officers were invited to enter the contest.

Over the years, the Nations Cup changed and the competitions were opened up to civilians. By 1949, it was only Ireland that still insisted on military teams for the Nations Cup in Dublin. Finally, in the early 1950s, FEI rules were drawn up and these govern the Nations Cup regulations today.

The scoring system

Four riders, male or female, military or civilian, make up each team. They must

ride round a course of jumps twice, but only the best three results from each round count toward the final total for the team as a whole.

This means that if one rider has a disastrous round, picking up perhaps 28 faults, and the other three all jump clear, the bad round can be discarded, and the team still has no faults.

The rider with the poor first round can go on to ride in the second. Again, one rider's faults can be discarded and not added to the final score.

If there is a draw between two teams, they must jump off against the clock to decide the winner.

Rules

The rules state that a show can ask only the six best placed teams from the first round to go forward to the second round.

This not only prevents the class from going on too long, it also means that when the remaining teams jump in reverse order of merit, the pressure and excitement are kept up till the end.

When the first Nations Cup was staged all those years ago, there was nothing to stop a country holding more than one Cup during the season.

Nowadays – with the exception of very large countries such as the USA – each country is only allowed to stage one per season. At least three teams must take part in the competition for it to be recognized as a Nations Cup. Those taking part can be either amateur or professional riders.

As well as the prestige of winning a Nations Cup, there is another goal for

▼ **Australia's** Vicky Roycroft and Apache take a fence at Aachen, Germany.

▲ **America's** Melanie Smith checks the height of a jump.

each country to aim at. Points are awarded to the top teams in every Nations Cup, six to the winner, four to the second, three to the third and so on. At the end of the year each country totals its six best results to find the overall champion of the Nations Cup Series.

The President's Cup

The results of major international championships as well as Nations Cups are taken into account in deciding the winner of the President's Cup. The really big competitions, such as the Olympic Games, count for more points.

World Final

An extra event took place in 1991. The seven leading countries from all over the world were invited to send teams to a World Final in Belgium. This competition, recently revived, is now called the Nations Trophy Series. It is to be held annually in September in varying locations.

◄ **Jump heights:** Under international rules, fences can be 1.4-1.6m (4ft 6in-5ft 2in) high. Klaus Reinacher of Germany takes the rails in his stride at Dublin in 1986.

◄**President Hillary,** former President of Ireland, proudly presents the Nations Cup to a winning Irish team at the Dublin Horse Show.

▼ **At Aachen** in Germany the American team won the 1987 Nations Cup. From left to right they are: Joe Fargis on Mill Pearl; Lisa Tarnopol on Revlon Adam; Anne Kursinski on Starman; and Joan Scharffenberger on Victor. Conrad Homfeld, Chef d'Equipe, is standing at the front.

▲ **Areas** are set aside for warming-up and daily exercise during the week. There is also a collecting ring with practice jumps.

▼ **Organizers** brief the arena staff between events, so everyone knows what they should be doing. The gates in the centre of the picture are where competitors enter the main arena.

▲ **Blacksmiths** are on call to deal with any unexpected shoeing.

► **Hidden** from public view are stores at either side of the arena — as well as underneath the Royal box! Plants and jumps are kept here.

Backstage at Wembley

The Horse of the Year Show is a highlight of October for the horse world. It takes place at Wembley Arena in London, and although it lasts for just five days, work goes on throughout the year for the show director and his team.

Stables in the car park

The really big build-up starts the month before the show itself. This is when the arena car park is transformed: 500 stables are built in neat rows to house some of 1000 horses that will arrive to take part.

More than 200 of the horses – from mighty Shires to speedy Pony Club contestants – are 'residents' here for the entire week of the show. Others stay for a day or two, while another 100 more come in each day for different classes. Grooms, competitors, and trade-stand holders live in a village of caravans and horseboxes just near the stables.

Perfect soil mix

The week after the stables are started, the immense task of laying the soil in the arena begins. This is a highly specialized job, as the depth and content of the soil must be exactly right for show jumping. The same mix is used each year, and takes two days to lay down. It is made of sand, soil, gravel and saw-

WAITING IN THE WINGS

The timing of the whole event has to be precise. Competitors in the class following the one currently in the arena have to assemble in the outer collecting ring.

When their class begins, the first two are called to an inner ring. Then they are called one by one. This way there are always two competitors waiting their turn.

◄ **Without** good organization there would be traffic jams and chaos. Teams of stewards direct display teams and entrants, making sure everyone is in the right place at the right time.

▼ **The arena party** is highly trained, repairing and dismantling jumps at top speed. They have diagrams to help them, and the course builders are there with measuring tapes and sticks to make sure the jumps are accurate.

▲ The Ring Guard blows a hunting horn to signal the start of each class.

▼ Members of the Oakleigh Pony Club set off to practise for the mounted games class.

dust, and over 1000 tons (1016 tonnes) are needed! The job takes at least two days, and afterwards the mix is returned to the warehouse to be stored for the following year.

In the last few days before the show, stable managers and vets, course builders and timekeepers, arrive to check equipment. There are also commentators, doctors and the invaluable stewards to be briefed. Some of the stewards take a week's holiday from their usual jobs so they can be there.

Warming up

There are two collecting rings for competitors – the outer one is the biggest, and is housed in a marquee with two practice jumps in it. Here you can see all types of horses – from small ponies to heavy horses – being quietly exercised and warmed up.

The jumps are raised and lowered constantly, making hard work for the helpers. The ring becomes full, but practice jumping carries on regardless. Competitors have to keep a sharp eye on other horses. When the trumpeters of the Household Cavalry are tuning up, for example, many horses object!

▼ Arena commentators have a stressful job. They must research details about the competitors, and always sound calm.

◄ **Despite the frenzy** as they wait between the two collecting rings, the horses still manage to look beautifully turned out.

▼ **Merseyside police horses** form part of the force's display and contend for the title 'Best Police Horse of the Year'.

Anyone for Badminton?

Every year, the most famous three-day event in the world transforms a quiet corner of England into the home of a crowded and spectacular show. It draws more people than almost any other international sporting occasion: it is the Badminton Horse Trials!

A part of history

The sport of eventing has its roots in training exercises for the cavalry and, even today, it tests the three qualities desired of a cavalry horse: obedience, speed, and reliability. The Badminton Trials, which were first held in 1949, challenge these qualities to the full.

The course is designed by Colonel Weldon who himself won Badminton twice in earlier years. His experience as a competitor is reflected in the ingenious courses he designs – always fair to the horses but demanding the highest possible skill from their riders.

The cross-country course takes in a number of permanent features, like the notorious Irish Bank, as well as a series of simpler jumps that ensure no two Badmintons are ever the same!

◄ **Badminton** attracts some of the largest crowds for any sporting event in the world. The Duke of Beaufort owns the Avon estate where the championships are held.

◄ **Lucinda Green** and Willy B prepare for the cross country. Lucinda gained her first Badminton title in 1973 and won a record five more times in the next 10 years.

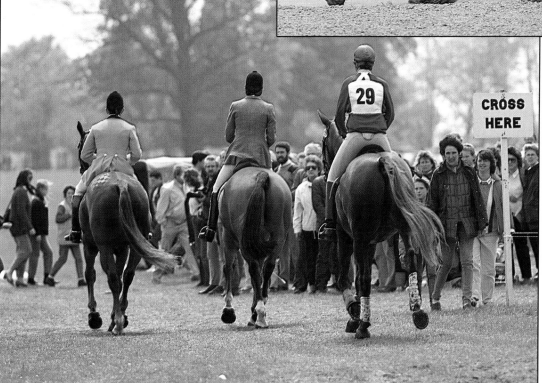

▲ **On the Sunday** of the weekend event all competitors parade for the crowds.

CROSS HERE

◄ **A competitor** is escorted by stewards to the start of the road test section. Being on horseback gives the stewards a big advantage: they can see over people's heads and spot any likely problems that may arise with the traffic.

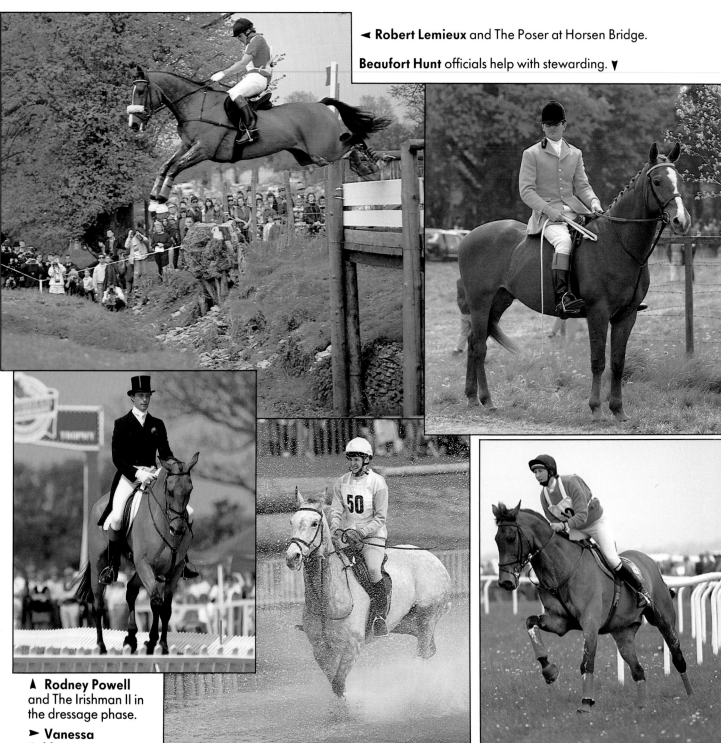

◀ **Robert Lemieux** and The Poser at Horsen Bridge.

Beaufort Hunt officials help with stewarding. ▼

▲ **Rodney Powell** and The Irishman II in the dressage phase.

➤ **Vanessa Ashbourne** and Hector James tackle the Lake Jump.

The power of three

As with all other three-day events, Badminton is made up of three phases. Dressage is the first phase, cross country is the second and show jumping is the third and last.

The highlight of Badminton is the cross country in phase two, but the course is only part of several sections that day. Competitors begin by riding along 4km (almost 2½ miles) of marked roads and tracks which they must complete within a strict time limit. This is followed by a steeplechase which must be covered in four-and-a-half minutes. The run is 3km (nearly 2 miles) long, with six small brush jumps. Without stopping, the entrants then continue on to another speed trial over 10km (6 miles) of roads and tracks.

After this comes a rest period and compulsory veterinary inspection to check the horses for signs of exhaustion, lameness or injury.

The main course

Only those that are passed fit are allowed to continue on to the cross country, which is the final section of the second phase.

The horses and riders tackle an ex-

► **Clarissa Strachan** and Master Fiddler clear the Wood Pile.

▼ **Whitbread Shires** join the grand parade.

▲ **Virginia Leng** on Master Craftsman at the ski-jump.

◄ **Angela Tucker** and Good Value in the steeplechase.

tremely challenging course 7km (4 miles) long, peppered with daunting obstacles that must be jumped at speed to avoid time penalties.

A fence judge and assistant stand at each jump to check on competitors and record any faults they may incur. Stewards from the Beaufort Hunt are also on hand to oversee the riders and help with crowd control.

The course twists and bends through the most complicated and varied countryside possible, with high jumps, wide jumps, combinations, ascents, descents and water jumps.

The water jumps are particularly difficult for the horses who have no way of telling how deep the water might be. But they are very popular with the public, who are secretly hoping that at least one competitor will take an untimely bath!

▲ **Ian Stark** won Badminton in 1986, and completely stole the limelight two years later when he came both first and second — the only rider to have achieved this. He won on his big bay Sir Wattie, and was second on Glenburnie.

Riders are only allowed to compete on two horses in the Trials, although most entrants take more horses with them.

◄ **Tinks Pottinger** on Volunteer clears the last fence in the show-jumping phase.

133

Show with a Royal setting

The Royal Windsor Show held every May is much loved by the horse world. It was first organized in 1943 – during the Second World War – to raise funds for the war effort. Although that first event was only a small gymkhana, the Windsor Show has grown to be a huge international attraction.

Today it is the only open-air show in Britain where so many kinds of event are represented. Spread over the dressage and three show rings, you can see working hunters, Grade 'A' show jumpers, heavy horses and dainty show ponies. A popular attraction is the driving course, introduced to the show by Prince Philip. The show is so vast that runners on horseback are needed to collect the results and take them to the show secretary's office. Pony Club members act as runners. The show setting is magnificent – Windsor Home Park, The Royal grounds next to Windsor Castle. No wonder it has been called the garden party of the showing calendar!

► **Members** of mounted units from all branches of the Services have a chance to test their jumping skills. They ride in uniform in teams of three, and the team with the least number of faults wins.

▲ **The Queen** presents a cup to the best turned-out Trooper. Judging is based on turn-out during the previous three months, and not just at the show itself.

▲ **All breeds** and colours can be seen at Windsor, like these unusual palomino Shetlands.

◄ **A scenic** route along the River Thames makes warming up before a driving class all the more enjoyable.

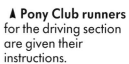

▲ **Pony Club runners** for the driving section are given their instructions.

▼ **Ponies on parade:** The owner of this beautifully turned-out show pony makes him stand out for the judge. The pony's outline is enhanced by quarter markings and shark's teeth.

▶ **The Band** of the Household Cavalry prepares to strike up a tune, led by the drum horse Caractacus, who stands 17 hands high.

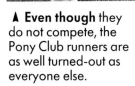

▲ **Pretty in pink:** This elegant pair in the side-saddle class waits hopefully for the judge's verdict.

▲ **Even though** they do not compete, the Pony Club runners are as well turned-out as everyone else.

▶ **Competitors** for the Driving Grand Prix come from all over Europe and as far away as North America to take part. This handsome grey gelding is from Switzerland.

◄ **Police horses** are on show as well as being on duty. There is a class for the best-trained mount, and entrants are drawn from forces all over Britain.

▼ **Between duties,** runners can relax and soak up the early summer sunshine.

Welsh Cobs come in all solid colours, including palomino. A flowing mane and forelock are characteristic.

The Royal Welsh Show

The Royal Welsh is one of the top agricultural shows in Great Britain, and lasts for four days. It takes place every summer at its showground near Builth Wells, a mid-Wales market town.

Welsh people are particularly proud of their horses. The breeds are divided into four sections, A to D. A is the smallest and is the popular Welsh Mountain Pony, Section D is the largest and stockiest. All are regarded as intelligent and strong, and are widely used for cross as well as pure-breeding.

Wales is horse country, where the rolling landscape is ideal for hacking and trekking. Horses have always been a part of working life, too. Sheep farmers still ride the Welsh pony when they round up their flocks.

◄ **A crested neck** and muscular quarters are typical of all Welsh sections. This pony is Section A, under 12 hands.

▲ **These Suffolk Punches** have travelled the width of England to take part in a display at the show's main ring.

Many breeds — besides the Welsh ones — can be seen at the show.

◄ **Welsh-bred ponies** take part in the private drive class. Judges look for correct gait and conformation.

▲ **The show jumping** attracts many breeds and cross-breeds. Ponies crossed with Welsh blood inherit good balance and strong limbs.

► **Chestnut and bay** are colours often found among Section Bs, which must be under 13.2 hands. This proud stallion came first in his class.

◄ **The Section D** Welsh Cob stallions draw the greatest crowds at the show. There is no upper height limit on these fiery horses, though most grow no higher than 15.2 hands.

► **The show** is spread over a huge area, and includes three rings and hundreds of small pavilions.

▼ **A judge** puts a Section D Cob through its paces. Welsh ponies are versatile. They make good family riding animals, and are also excellent in harness.

The Sydney Show

The Sydney Royal Easter Show is the biggest of its kind in Australia, and lasts for 11 days. Apart from the livestock and agricultural events, there are more than 350 classes for horses and ponies. Among the breeds on show are the Australian Thoroughbred and the Galloway, and there are competitions for every discipline – from trotting races to show jumping, team riding and polo matches.

The Royal Agricultural showground has a special stable block, and nearby Centennial Park provides plenty of space to exercise.

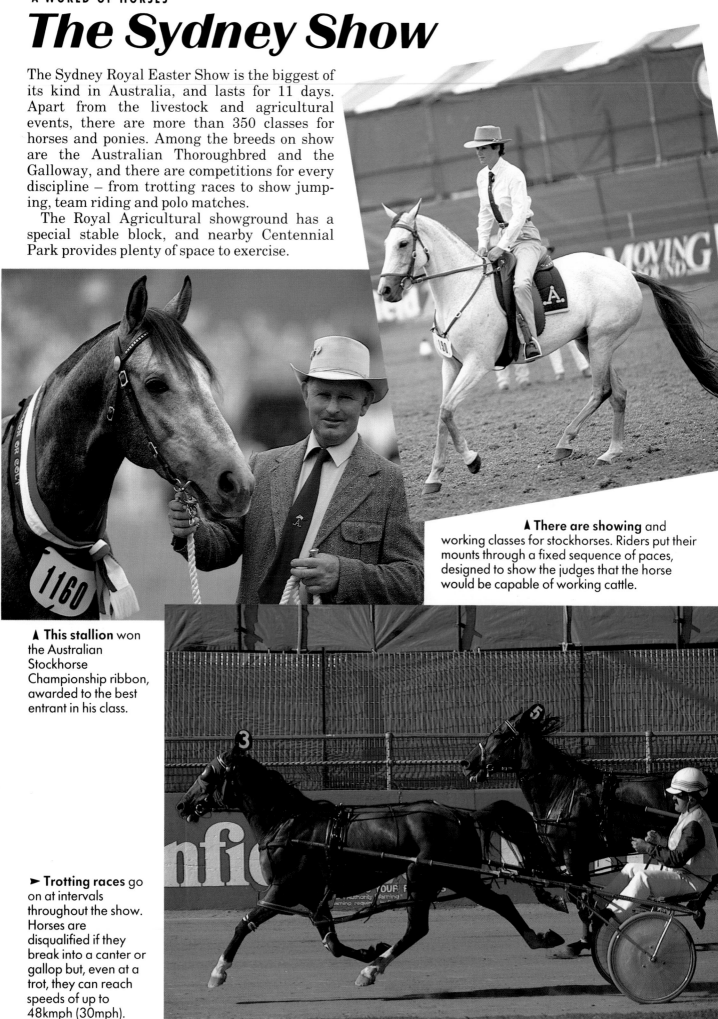

▲ **There are showing** and working classes for stockhorses. Riders put their mounts through a fixed sequence of paces, designed to show the judges that the horse would be capable of working cattle.

▲ **This stallion** won the Australian Stockhorse Championship ribbon, awarded to the best entrant in his class.

► **Trotting races** go on at intervals throughout the show. Horses are disqualified if they break into a canter or gallop but, even at a trot, they can reach speeds of up to 48kmph (30mph).

◄ **The New South Wales Mounted Artillery** show off their horsemanship in a drill performed by teams of four. The flags are designed to match their uniform.

► **All age groups** are catered for. After performing their show for the judge in a riding pony class, these two take time to have a look around.

▲ **Teams** take part in tent-pegging competitions. At full gallop, the riders aim a lance at tent pegs driven into the ground and try to carry them away. They win points if they succeed in 'stabbing' a peg and scooping it off, but waste their go if they miss!

◄ **A team of four** makes its way to the arena. The competitors are all riding Galloways, a breed of small horse that stands between 14.2 and 15 hands high. The Galloway is a popular Pony Club mount in Australia.

◄ Horses and ponies pulling trade vehicles provide a colourful display. Prize-winning cattle are on view in the background.

▼ A Clydesdale is walked out for showing in-hand. Typical of the breed are the many, large white markings and splendid feather. The mane and tail are decorated in a show-style often used for draught horses.

▼ Rangers are always on duty in Centennial Park and, when the Sydney Show is on, they help with the stewarding. Everyone wears a hat to protect them from the sun, but the weather can change, and the sunhat ends up keeping off the rain!

► The New South Wales Mounted Artillery forms a Guard of Honour for a member of the Royal Family.

▲ **After** the hectic whirl of showing, this Stud Book pony and her owner relax in the shade of Centennial Park. If the stabling is full, some horses are kept in the park overnight, while their owners camp out alongside to keep an eye on them.

▼ **There are three grand parades** in the main arena for all the winners. They form a continuous 'snake' so that the thousands of spectators in the grandstand have a chance to see them before the show ends.

▲ **The show is an important date** for the Australian horse world. It attracts the nation's top show jumpers, such as John Fahey on Focus.

▲ **Prize winners** take part in a grand parade in the afternoon, that leads them past all the grandstands.

◄ **A driving pony** is trotted out.

▼ **There's no mistaking** a touch of class in this Polish Arab stallion called Applause. He scooped up first place in the Saddle Pony event.

The Royal Canberra Show

Canberra, Australia's capital city, is the centre of great attention every February. It is then that the city hosts the Royal Show – an important date in the equine and agricultural calendar.

All breeds

Like big shows everywhere, the programme is full of all kinds of event. There are classes for cattle, sheep, pigs – even goats! For horse-lovers, of course, the real treat is to see the wide range of breeds, all beautifully turned out.

Horses and riders from all over the country flock to Canberra for the weekend. But before horses can qualify to take part in the show, they must win prizes at the smaller local shows.

The main attractions are the highly trained stockhorses, and the Clydesdales, who in pioneer days were invaluable in helping to clear the land.

The Royal Canberra is a particularly big event in the Pony Club calendar, with a large contingent from all parts of Australia taking part in competitions and games.

◄ **In-hand Shetlands** are led past a class of Palominos who are lined up waiting to be judged.

▼ **The mounted stewards** are easily spotted by their bright red coats. One of their duties is to lead entrants into the ring at the start of their class.

►**A Galloway mare** joins the grand parade.
The breed was developed in Australia.

▼ **Time to unplait** before heading home.

◄ **Pony Club** teams are colour co-ordinated. The Zone number refers to the area where they live.

► **Hosing** helps to keep the horses cool.

▼ **As the day** draws to a close, working stockhorses make their way back to their horseboxes.

Young Clydesdales wait to take part in the yearling in-hand class. Their headcollars are made from hemp, which is traditionally used when showing this breed. Clydesdales are gentle and affectionate.

Michael Matz, a top American show jumper, schools one of his novice horses at the West Palm Beach equestrian centre.

Florida: Sunshine showground

The state of Florida has long been famous for its beautiful weather, sandy beaches and Disney World. More recently, however, the 'Sunshine State' has blossomed into a major equestrian centre that attracts top-class competitors from all over the world. Whether the sport is show jumping, flat racing, harness racing, drag hunting or polo, sunny Florida is the perfect venue.

Show jumping in the sun

Because Florida is a southern state, the climate is very mild. While Europe is suffering the winter cold, the temperatures there are quite warm. This is one of the reasons Florida has become part of the international show-jumping circuit. Grand Prix and World Cup qualifiers can be held there from December to April.

Major competitions take place at per-

USA
Tampa
West Palm Beach
Pompano Beach   Miami

◄ **One of the six show rings** – complete with swaying palm trees – at West Palm Beach. The ground has to be watered daily to keep it moist and maintain good footing.

▼ **Each morning** at the Pompano Harness Track the horses are put through their training paces. The public is welcome to watch them as they exercise. The races take place at night under bright lights.

manent showgrounds in West Palm Beach and Tampa. The West Palm Beach centre has six show rings and a stable block that can house 1500 horses. Tampa's Bob Thomas Equestrian Centre can accommodate 800 horses and in 1989 it hosted the Volvo World Cup, which was won by Canada's Ian Millar and Big Ben.

Racing for everyone

Florida has much to offer the racing fan. It is home to four Thoroughbred race tracks, one Quarter Horse track and a harness track. Most of the horses that compete in the races are bred in the United States.

Gulfstream Park near Miami is open during the winter months when Thoroughbred racing takes place six days and nights a week! It has a dirt track as well as a grass one and is completely flat.

The Pompano Harness Track at Pompano Beach is known as the Winter Capital of Harness Racing. Over the years this race track has played host to many of harness racing's international cham-

pions, including the legendary Niatross, who in 1980 became the sport's first 2 million dollar winner.

Hot weather hunting

Hunting is fast becoming a popular sport in Florida. As wild foxes are rare in the Sunshine State, the Palm Beach Hunt is a drag hunt. The hunt starts early in the morning to avoid the intense heat of the afternoon. All the fences have to be specially made because the farm land the hunt rides over is open and has no natural hedges or walls.

Palm trees and polo

Just round the corner from the West Palm Beach showground is the Polo and Country Club, which is home to polo's World Cup championship. It attracts the best polo players in the world – among them many international celebrities. It is quite normal to see several nine or ten goal players (ten is the highest rating a polo player can have) participate in the same action-packed match.

▼ **Gulfstream Park** is just outside Miami in southern Florida. Up to 10 races are held here each day. The race track is flat all the way round – unlike many racecourses in Britain, where the last stretch is run up a slope.

▲ **Drag hunting** in Florida takes place early in the morning – starting at 8am – to avoid the heat later on in the day. The riders wear traditional hunting clothes and start the day with a welcoming stirrup cup.

Overleaf: American show jumper Anne Kurzinski pops a horse over a practice fence in the warming-up arena of the West Palm Beach showground.

◄**The West Palm Beach Polo and Country Club** attracts the best polo players in the world and is home to polo's World Cup championship.

Trot on!

Harness racing is the modern version of ancient chariot racing, but while the Greeks and Romans galloped their horses, today's races are at a trot. The American Standardbred was the first horse to be specially bred for the sport. It is mainly Thoroughbred but with an added mix of Morgan, Arab and Hackney stock.

Strict paces

Harness races are popular throughout the world, and while countries have different race rules, all are strict about pace. A horse is penalized if he breaks into a canter or gallop, and in some cases is automatically placed last.

There may be many reasons why a horse breaks his gait: he may be over-excited, tired, or his step could have become unbalanced. This is why good training is so important.

Training a winner

Trotters show potential even as foals, when they can be seen practising their gait. A trainer also looks for a young horse with good straight conformation. A trotter's work load is strenuous –

much tougher than a young racehorse's – so racers do not begin until they are three years old.

Great patience and careful handling are needed to teach the horse to contain his best speed at the trot and to keep in gait. There are two recognized gaits:

▼ **Pacing races** are run at Australia's biggest show, the Royal Sydney. Down under, the vehicles are known as sulkies.

▼ **The races** can be run on a grass or hard track. The distance is usually 1.6km (1 mile). The horses are warmed up on a practice circuit just before the start.

pacers trot with the legs on one side moving together, while trotters move on the diagonal.

A racer's work is built up daily – a mixture of fast work, jogging and road work. This ensures the horses reach a peak of fitness for the season's start.

In the driving seat

There are *ridden* trotting races in France, but harness races are more common elsewhere. The racing carriage has different names around the world: in Britain it is called a cart, in America and Australia the vehicle is a sulky, but it is also known as a buggy or bike.

Drivers sit with their feet in fixed stirrups, and have no leg or seat aids like jockeys, so the main means of communication is through the reins.

And they're off!

When the horses are under starter's orders, a car-mounted gate the width of the track drives ahead to keep the racers in line. As soon as they cross the starting line, the car picks up speed and moves ahead out of their way.

The race is usually two circuits of the track, and stewards posted at regular intervals keep a strict check that no horse breaks out of a trot.

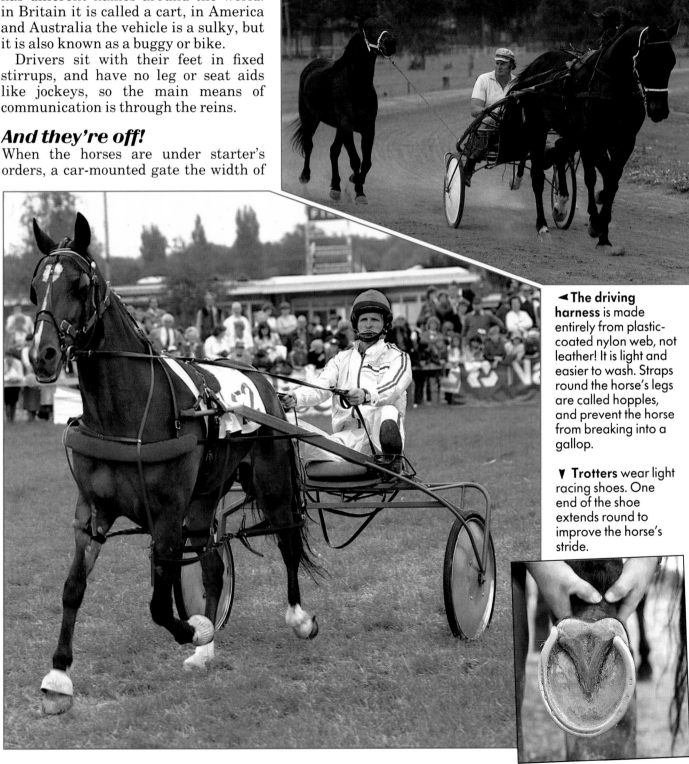

▼ **The Australian State** of New South Wales is well-known for breeding trotters and pacers. Here, a trainer leads two young horses to get them used to the sulky.

◄ **The driving harness** is made entirely from plastic-coated nylon web, not leather! It is light and easier to wash. Straps round the horse's legs are called hopples, and prevent the horse from breaking into a gallop.

▼ **Trotters** wear light racing shoes. One end of the shoe extends round to improve the horse's stride.

◄ **Red Mile** is a famous American race track in Lexington, Kentucky.

There are two types of racing breeds — pacers and trotters. In this picture they are racing together: the horse on the left is a trotter, as he is moving on the diagonal; his opponent is trotting on the lateral (the pair of legs on one side moving together).

The pacer is wearing a sheepskin noseband to discourage him from putting his head in the air.

DID YOU KNOW?
Foam plugs placed in the horses' ears blot out the noise of the crowds and keep the racers calm before the start of a race.

The earplugs are attached to the reins and bridle and once the race has begun, the driver can release them to get his horse going.

Hats off to Ascot!

Royal Ascot is the grandest of all the race meetings. It starts on a Tuesday in mid-June, and is the most popular four days of the flat-racing season, as well as one of the highlights of the social calendar.

Royal presence

Ascot is the only racecourse owned by the British Crown, and the popularity it enjoys is down to the continued support of members of the Royal Family. They enjoy the meeting in an area closed off from the general public. This is called the Royal Enclosure.

To be allowed in, applications must be sent to the Queen's Representative. Two references are needed from Royal Enclosure Members of at least seven years' standing, and only distinguished people are chosen.

But as well as prestige, Ascot offers one of the best racing turfs in the world. The type of ground over which races are run is very important. Like all horses, Thoroughbreds can damage their legs

▲ **Royal Ascot** is as famous for hats as for racing. While gentlemen wear the top hat variety, ladies enjoy wearing ones that stand out in the crowd. The Thursday of Ascot week is Ladies' Day, and this is when fashion designers enjoy the chance to go over the top!

▼ **Winning horses,** and those placed second and third, are allowed into the unsaddling enclosure. There the public can see them before the horses are led away to the racecourse stables.

FIRST

by too much fast work over hard terrain. Waterlogged ground is just as unsuitable, because the horses have to work harder, and risk straining their tendons.

Ascot offers just the right conditions. There are two courses, one circular and the other straight, and both are built on well-drained soil.

Glittering prizes

A total of 24 races are run at the meeting – six per day. Tuesday, the opening day at Ascot, is considered by some to be the best day's racing. The first race is always the Queen Anne Stakes, named after the Queen who founded the course in 1711. It attracts a high-class field of runners, including Europe's best horses over a mile.

British trainer Henry Cecil enjoyed considerable success with this event – saddling four different winners in a row from 1981.

Another highlight on the first day is the Prince of Wales Stakes run over a mile (nearly 2km). Trainers use it as a

▼ **The standard** of racing at Ascot has remained supreme, and some of the most famous racehorses, such as Nijinsky and Shergar, have made their name there.

stepping stone for other major races that are held during the summer.

Later in the first day is the St James' Palace Stakes. The race is only open to three-year-olds. It is always well supported by leading trainers.

The Royal meeting also stages the King Edward VII Stakes, known as the Ascot Derby. Horses who may have run the Derby at Epsom but been unplaced, have a chance to tackle the Ascot race instead.

But without doubt the most important race staged at Ascot is run at the end of July, a month after the Royal meeting. This is called Diamond Day, and is when the King George VI and Queen Eliza-beth Diamond Stakes is run over 1½ miles (2.4km). Legendary names have won the King George, including Mill Reef, Reference Point and Mtoto.

The race ranks as one of the top in England, because it comes at a time when racehorses are at their peak. A horse who proves himself in this race is likely to do well for the rest of the season. Breeders keep a keen eye out for additions to their studs.

A ladies-only race is run that day too – the Ladies' Diamond Stakes. It balances the fact that male jockeys still dominate the sport. Princess Anne won it in 1987, and was greeted by her family in the winner's enclosure!

► **The Royal meeting** attracts the largest crowd of the sporting summer season.

▼ **Royal jockey** Willie Carson has always enjoyed great public support at Ascot.

◄ **The Royal Family,** conveyed by carriage, traditionally opens each day's meeting. The Crown Prince of Saudi Arabia, Sheik Abdullah, is pictured here with the Queen and Prince Philip.

▼ **The best races** have 'Stakes' in their titles. 'Stake' was the word for prize money, in the days when amateur owners raced their horses against each other.

Churchill Downs

Churchill Downs' twin spires are recognized by racing fans all over the world. The huge grandstand seats 52,000 people and is home to the exclusive Turf Club and terraced area that has been nicknamed 'Millionaires' Row'.

The state of Kentucky produces some of the best racehorses in the world. It is also home to the famous Churchill Downs racecourse. Situated in the city of Louisville, Churchill Downs has, since 1875, played host to the most important flat race in the United States – the Kentucky Derby.

A course for a colonel

In 1865, Colonel M Lewis Clarke decided that the bustling city of Louisville needed a race-track. Colonel Clarke travelled to Europe to study stakes races and the rules governing the sport. He was most impressed by the English system of racing and therefore decided to use it as the model for his own races back in Louisville.

When he returned to Kentucky, Clarke leased some land from his uncles, John and Henry Churchill. In 1874 he built a race-track on the land and a huge grandstand with two distinctive spires. He named his new track the Louisville Jockey Club and a year later, in front of 10,000 cheering spectators, the first Kentucky Derby was run.

A three-year-old colt named Aristides won the race, which has earned the nickname the 'Run for the Roses' because the winning horse is blanketed with a garland of roses and the jockey is given a beautiful bouquet.

This fragrant tradition began in 1883 when all the ladies who attended the Derby were given a red rose at a party after the race. Colonel Clarke liked this idea and adopted the rose as the track's official flower.

New owners

Clarke sold the Jockey Club in 1894 to a group of wealthy Louisville businessmen. They set about tearing down the old grandstand and replacing it with a bigger one on the opposite side of the track – to protect racing fans from the glare of the afternoon sun.

In 1902 a Louisville tailor, Matt J Winn, took over the running of the track. As a child Winn had watched the very first Derby from the seat of his father's grocery wagon. Now an ardent racing enthusiast, he persuaded local businessmen to invest more money in the track and rebuild the clubhouse.

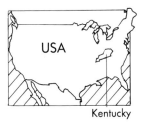
USA
Kentucky

▼ In the Turf Club garden, visitors can watch the racing results on a big toteboard or admire the bronze statue of Aristides – the first horse to win the Kentucky Derby.

The garden is full of colourful flowers that are planted so they bloom in May – just in time for the Derby.

The track changed its name to Churchill Downs – a combination of the name of the course's original owners and the English word for grassy land. This new track was a success and attracted racing fans from all over Kentucky.

A track for today

Today Churchill Downs covers 57 hectares (140 acres). The sprawling grandstand and luxurious clubhouse seat more than 50,000 people. On big race days the course attracts over 130,000 visitors. Much of the crowd walk through tunnels underneath the track that lead them to the huge infield. These enthusiastic racing fans set up elaborate picnics and thoroughly enjoy themselves in the party-like atmosphere.

The course has a huge stable area, with jockeys' quarters, fire-resistant tack rooms and 48 barns – enough room for 1350 horses! Six of the barns look out on to the 2km (1 mile) dirt race-track used annually for the Kentucky Derby.

The newest addition to Churchill

▲ **Trainers gallop** their horses on the 2km (1 mile) dirt track on the morning of the race. As well as being good practice for the horses, this helps them become familiar with the layout of the track.

►**The most talented** three-year-old Thoroughbreds in the world line up for the 1987 Kentucky Derby. A big bay colt named Alysheba galloped past the 17 other horses to win the 113th running of the race.

Downs is a grass track, which enabled the course to stage The Breeder's Cup in 1988. Now an annual event, the Breeder's Cup attracts the best turf horses from the USA, England, Ireland and France.

Derby days

Held on the first Saturday in May, the Kentucky Derby is the first and most important of three American Classic races for three year olds – known collectively as the Triple Crown. The other two are the Preakness Stakes in Maryland and the Belmont Stakes in New York. If a horse wins all three races, he instantly becomes a huge celebrity and is worth vast sums of money.

Secretariat, a big playful chestnut colt out of Bold Ruler, won all three races in 1973 and became the first Triple Crown winner for 25 years. He was the track favourite and set a speed record for the race that still stands today. Many racing fans think that Secretariat was *the* horse of the century.

◄ **Nowadays** more than 130,000 people attend the Derby and an estimated 20 million racing fans throughout the world watch the race on the television or listen to it on the radio.

▼ **Winning Colors,** shown here wearing number eight, made history twice over when she won the 1988 Derby. She became only the third filly in racing history to capture the Derby and the only roan ever to win the race.

The story of polo

▲ **Shoe studs** (called 'calkins') are fitted to hind shoes to prevent the pony from slipping.

▲ **Stick grip:** A sling goes around the back of the hand and thumb to give support.

▲ **The stick head** is fixed to the stick at an angle so the ball can be hit out and away by the player.

Polo developed as a way of keeping men and horses fit for combat. It is one of the oldest games in the world. The earliest record of it goes right back to Ancient Persia in the sixth century BC.

How the game developed

Polo spread from Tibet to India from about 1600 onward. Indeed, the name 'polo' probably comes from the Tibetan language: 'Pu-lu' or 'Po-lo' was the name of the willow root from which the ball was made.

In the 19th century when Queen Victoria was on the throne, British colonialists in India encountered polo and introduced it to European riders. The first match was played in England between the 10th Hussars and the 9th Lancers on Hounslow Heath, outside London, in 1871.

The game was introduced into Argentina which soon became the biggest breeder and exporter of polo ponies. Argentinian players, too, are highly thought of.

How to play

Polo has been called hockey on horseback, and the two games are similar. Two teams with four players each must score goals between opposite goalposts.

A match is broken up into 'chukkas', a word which comes from the Hindi 'cakkar' meaning 'a round'. Each chukka lasts seven and a half minutes. There is a maximum of six chukkas in the United Kingdom, but four is more usual.

Two mounted umpires and a referee oversee play. The match begins with the two teams lined up at the centre of the pitch, opposite their opponents. The umpire throws in the ball and, when a goal is scored, the teams change ends.

The ponies

Professional players prefer to ride Thoroughbreds because of their stamina and speed, but a calm temperament is as valuable as breeding.

Courage is important, and a polo pony must be able to gallop flat out, swing round in a pirouette, and set off at top speed from a standstill.

◄ **Polo** is an exciting sport and both players and ponies need protection. As well as knee pads and a special hat, notice how one player has taken the added precaution of wearing a face visor – a safety device favoured by Prince Charles, who was an avid player for many years.

▼ **Team colours** are optional. The Lifeguards, however, are an eye-catching side: they match their ponies' bandages with their own red and blue outfits.

There is a current shortage of high-class polo trainers. Basic training is a little different from that of other riding horses, and takes two years from a pony's breaking-in. The three main movements a pony must learn are to change legs and to alter balance at the slightest indication; to stop and start instantly he is asked; and to turn on his haunches.

The player

Players hold the reins in one hand, and turn the pony by neck-reining: they move the rein hand in the direction intended, together with usual leg aids.

The player wears a special polo hat, and pads protect the knees against knocks. Brown boots and white breeches are required for formal matches.

The polo stick is usually measured in inches and is 48-53 inches in length

⋀ Once a male-dominated sport, polo is now enjoyed by an increasing number of women players. Pictured above is Victoria Grace playing for the La Manga team with opponent Rob Walton of the Maple Leafs.

➤ When not preparing to strike the ball, a player holds the stick up and away from the pony's legs.

Polo is a team game, and it is not considered good play to chase the ball for personal glory. A skilled player is one who passes the ball to a fellow team member if that player has a better chance of scoring.

Opposite page, top: 'Marking' your opponent is one of the keys to good polo-playing. Each team member has his equivalent on the opposing side, and it is his task to prevent his opponent from scoring a goal.

(120-135cm). The head is set at right angles in a 'T'-shape. It is made from bamboo, ash or sycamore. The white polo ball is 3½ inches in diameter (about 8.5cm). Traditionally it was made from bamboo or willow root, but nowadays it is plastic.

The tack

Leg bandages are essential to protect ponies from injury, and the tail is tied up to prevent it getting caught.

A breastplate keeps the saddle from slipping during play, and a standing martingale is essential: in the excitement of the game, even the best of horses could accidentally throw up his head and injure his rider.

Although there are no hard and fast rules about bitting, a plain Pelham (sometimes with the bottom rein alone) or a gag-snaffle are common.

High fliers

▼ **The horses** are put in their stalls before being loaded into the belly of the plane. The handlers work with horses all the time, and know how to care for them.

Competition horses are as well travelled as human celebrities! With so many international shows, the horses need to become used to transport by air as well as by road.

VIP treatment

Trained handlers look after the horses much as air stewardesses do their passengers! Regular checks are made to ensure that the horses have enough food and water. Because the temperature drops inside the aircraft, chills can be a real threat. Blankets are usually put on the horses to keep them warm.

The horses stand throughout their journey, tethered by headcollars. They would be more vulnerable if they were

lying down in their stalls, and the aeroplane swerved suddenly.

Tranquillizers may be given to the horses to calm them down. Rules on drug-use are strict for travelling animals, and in any case it could make them too dopey to compete well at their destination.

Horsy papers

Each horse has its own 'passport'. Instead of a photograph, there is an accurate drawing to show the horse's markings. Written details inside include the horse's name, its sire and dam, and a list of its vaccinations. Generally, though, the horses do not need new vaccinations before they go.

Health checks are important, and they are made before the horses leave, and again when they arrive at their destination. In Britain, for example, a Ministry of Agriculture vet examines all the horses before they leave, and fills out a health certificate. They cannot travel without this.

The vet looks for infectious diseases in particular, such as ringworm, coughs and colds. If he thinks a horse is unwell, he can stop it travelling.

Confined to quarters

It is mostly easy for horses to travel internationally. Some countries, however, have strict quarantine rules for horses arriving there.

During the quarantine period, horses are stabled in a separate area near the airport for anything between two and 21 days. They are tested during their stay to make sure they carry no infectious diseases that may be dangerous to other horses. Their grooms stay to look after them, and to give them exercise daily.

Happy travellers

Unlike some of their riders, the horses do not suffer 'jet lag' from their journey immediately. Instead, they usually begin to notice a change in diet, air and general surroundings a week or so after their journey.

But the horses rarely have a chance to reach that stage! If there are no quarantine restrictions, they are transported one or two days before their competitions start to give them just enough time for settling in. And those taking part in three-day events are on their way home before any jet lag has a chance to take hold.

YOUNG JET-SETTERS
Foals are allowed to travel as soon as they are strong enough! They are kept with their dam during the flight.

▼ ► **Sometimes** they are led up a gangway and loaded individually. Top competition horses who travel a lot usually find it easier to adjust to flying.

► **The horses** are well protected from possible injury. They wear leg bandages and knee pads. Poll guards prevent bruising in case they throw their heads up.

▼ **The horses** are often less tired by the travelling than their riders!

► **Hay nets** keep the horses occupied. The animals are also fed bran mashes and light meals. Those going on longer journeys are fed extra helpings of electrolytes — a mixture of vitamins and minerals — to replace elements the horses sweat out.

Ski-whizz!

▼ The 'white turf' may be soft and powdery, but it requires greater effort on the part of the horse to cover ground. Strength and stamina are important qualities for a winter racer — and so is a liking for the feel of snow under his feet!

Horse racing on skis is a highly skilled and exciting sport. Known as _skikjoring_ (pronounced 'shi-shur-ring'), it involves Thoroughbred horses dragging skiers at full gallop over snow tracks.

From sleighs to skis

The sport started in St Moritz in Switzerland at the turn of the century. Some Englishmen living there wanted a bit of excitement and they had the idea of using sleigh horses to pull a skier rather than pulling a sleigh.

Over the years, competitors refined this system to increase their racing time. Faster horses were trained, the 'jockey' was abandoned, and skiers learnt to control their racers by using sleigh-length reins.

The sport became so popular with spectators that an official race season

was soon introduced, and today, St Moritz plays host to an international gathering of skikjoring enthusiasts.

Snow surface

Compared to turf, snow is a smoother but heavier track for the racehorses.

► **Early morning** is a good time for practice runs. There are few people about, and the beautiful alpine scenery looks its best.

Extra warm blankets and a hood protect the horses from the freezing cold. Everyone keeps a close eye on the weather: if the temperature rises, the race track starts to melt and could be too dangerous for racing.

▼ Between races competitors keep on the move to limber up and stay warm. Many find a quiet area away from the crowds to keep their highly strung horses calm.

While speeds reached are faster, the horse must have greater stamina so as not to tire easily.

Suitable entrants compete in heats, a limited number at a time, over a distance of about 2km (1½ miles). The five fastest race against each other in the final, which is held on the third day of the winter horse-racing events.

The thrill of watching skikjoring often begins days before the event. Horses and competitors train and exercise locally. On the day of the race itself, getting the horses ready at the starting line is not easy. Sometimes a commotion can break out when one of the horses decides to gallop off across the lake, and his skier is unable to stop him! To prevent this, stewards lead the spirited Thorough-

breds to the start of the race and quieten them down.

Official checks

There are strict rules to protect the skiers and the horses. The harnesses, reins and protective blankets are issued by the organizers and checked to make sure they are all of the same standard.

Helmets with vizors protect the skiers from the spray of snow and the chunks of ice that are thrown up by the horses' hooves. Brightly coloured skis were introduced so the horses could see and avoid them in the snow.

The competitors must be expert skiers, but success also depends on a complete understanding between man and horse.

▲ Extra warm blankets

▼ A flag-shaped sheet protects the driver's face from the frozen chunks kicked up by the horses' hooves.

▼ Staying in control can be difficult, especially if the horse gets over-excited. The racehorses can be any nationality, but must be over five years old.

◄ **Colourful clothing** helps to identify the competitors, and they can be spotted easily if they fall over in the snow.

THE NAME OF THE GAME

The name of the event, *skikjoring,* comes from the Norwegian verb 'to travel'. Spectators and hopeful entrants come to St Moritz from all over the world for the races. The spectacle has become a highlight of the European winter sporting scene.

★ **SAFETY SHOES**

As in all the horse-racing events that take place on the frozen St Moritz lake, the skikjoring horses wear special shoes. These have sharp studs screwed into them to give a sure grip on the slippery surface of snow and ice. All the equipment used in the race, including the size and quality of the shoes, must pass the strict requirements of the Swiss Horse Racing Association.

◄ **As soon as** the lake freezes solid, a track is marked out with railings. Grandstand seating ensures everyone watching gets a good view.

◄ **Horse and rider** develop a strong trust. Horseball requires the players to stretch up, lean down, even grapple for the ball, so riders rely on their horses to sense where they need to be.

► **The horses** become used to their riders being off-balance! An ordinary football is used, fitted with six leather handles so it can be picked up easily.

★ **RULES OF THE GAME**
☐ The team scoring the most goals wins.
☐ There are four horses and riders in each team: two extras are reserves.
☐ Before a goal is scored — by shooting the ball through the hoop — the ball must pass through the hands of three members of the same team.
☐ A player must not hold the ball for longer than ten seconds.
☐ Ill-treatment of horses both on and off the field is prohibited and the referee can penalize offenders. One rule, for example, states that it is strictly forbidden to hit a horse with the ball or slack of the reins.

Netball on horseback

There are few entertainments more exciting than a sports match on horseback. It's easy to think every kind of game has been invented, but the new team sport of horseball is spreading fast.

Team spirit

The game of horseball was started in France, and is rather like netball on horseback. The aim is to gain hold of the ball and shoot goals in the net.

The grass pitch on which it is played is almost twice the area of an ordinary netball court. There are four riders in a team, plus a referee on horseback, so with nine horses in action, more space is needed!

Cool and collected

The sport demands a particular kind of horse. Breeding, schooling and temperament are all important. A high level of fitness is also needed because, like polo, the game is made up of short bursts of action. So far, no horse has been specifically bred for the sport, but the Anglo-Arab and Andalusian have proved to be well suited. Both breeds are intelligent, small, and nimble – just the right qualities for the game.

Advanced schooling is needed. The horse has to perform half turns and flying changes, as well as sudden stops and quick bursts of speed. While most animals would be upset at the thought of a football flying past their ears, horseball horses learn to take it in ➤

▼ **The teams** always have a warm-up before the start of a match. During play, the riders must stand in their stirrups when they pass the ball. Often they drop both reins in the process — so obedient horses are essential.

their stride. A good mount develops 'ball sense', and knows that his rider wants to be where the ball is going.

Character is put to the test too. In the excitement of the match, the horses come into close contact with each other, and with other riders. So a tolerant and even-tempered horse is favoured.

Confident riders

Riders need to be able horsemen who can stay in control whatever the situation. Swooping down to pick the ball off the ground, and leaping up to catch it means the rider, like the horse, needs to be fit and supple. A sense of balance is vital, and ability to throw the ball and shoot goals is of course a plus!

Some trainers say that playing horseball is helpful even for *learner* riders. It's such fun chasing the ball that they forget to feel frightened!

▲ **The referees wear** different colours. One is mounted and the second is on foot. Only the team captains can dispute their decisions.

▼ **The good-tempered** and nimble Andalusian is a popular breed with horseball players. Horses must be at least four years old to take part.

► **The riders** cannot dismount during the match. Special stirrup straps attached to the girth support the riders, and allow them to lean down and retrieve the ball without falling off.

WELL-PROTECTED
Leg bandages and overreach boots protect the horses.

The players wear shoulder and knee pads, as well as a hard hat. The pace of horseball can get fast and furious!

▼ **Goal!** The net is mounted on a post 3m (10ft) high. The players must canter toward the goal post and shoot from a marked line.

The match is made up of two 10-minute halves.

Cut out for sport

▲During a cutting contest the rider cuts a calf from its herd and then loosens the reins and lets his horse take over. The cutting horse has to prevent the calf returning to the herd. If the rider is seen to aid the horse in any way he is given penalty points.

►Cutting horses are strong, nimble and quick. They have to be able to move lightly on their feet in the small arena.

Cutting has long been part of everyday ranching life for a cowboy. At the turn of this century, it became an organized sport, too. Today many riders in Australia and the USA keep a cutting horse simply for the fun of taking part in competitions.

Competitive cowboys

Working on a ranch, cowboys often have to cut out (separate) one calf from the herd, to brand, ear tag or wean it. Traditionally, cowboys are fiercely competitive about who has the best cutting horse – this is how cutting contests began. In the past they were informal events staged between rival ranchers. Nowadays the contests are governed by rules set down by the American Cutting Horse Association.

The right choice

At a cutting contest, horse and rider are confronted with 20 calves in an arena. They must enter the herd without ►

◄It takes much training to make a good cutting horse. Before the contest he is warmed up and put through the turns and stops that will be needed in the arena.

▼The cutting rider wears leather chaps, Western-style boots and hat. He can wear spurs but must not use them. Whips are not permitted.

A deep-seated Western cutting saddle is used by the rider and the horse has a simple bridle with no noseband.

▼ Cutting begins when horse and rider enter deep into the herd. The rider selects a calf that he thinks will provide his horse with the opportunity to show off its cutting skills. The horse then nudges the calf out into the centre of the arena without disturbing the rest of the herd.

dispersing it, cut out a calf and then prevent it rejoining the herd.

Each horse and rider has four assistants. Two are 'herd holders', who keep the calves near the back of the arena. The other two are 'turn-back men', who prevent the selected calf running away from the cutting horse.

Two judges watch and award the pair up to a maximum of 80 points. They also give penalties for any mistakes made.

A watchful eye

Once the rider has cut out his chosen calf, he lets the horse take over. He sits still, with the reins hanging loose in one hand and the other hand resting on the saddle horn. He keeps his legs well away from the horse's sides so that he isn't tempted to give leg aids – this would earn him penalties from the eagle-eyed judges.

Meanwhile the horse has to prevent the calf returning to the herd until the rider lifts the reins to take control again. An experienced horse works eye-to-eye with the calf, moving lightly to and fro, anticipating every movement the calf makes. He positions himself right in the middle of the arena for maximum control of the calf.

As soon as the rider senses his horse has complete control over the calf, he takes over again and tries to cut out a second calf. Top riders can tackle two or three animals in the allotted time of 2½ minutes. More points are given for two calves worked well than for three worked for a only a few seconds each.

Natural instincts

A good cutting horse loves his job and enjoys the process of outwitting the cattle. They are usually Quarter Horses or Appaloosas bred for their innate ability to understand how cows behave.

▲When the calf has been cut out, the rider sits still with his legs away from the horse so no leg aids can be given. The horse then keeps the calf from following its natural instinct and returning to the herd.

▼A well-trained cutting horse works eye-to-eye with the calf. If the calf steps to either side the horse moves even faster to keep it in position.

Cutting horses are intelligent animals with the natural ability to predict how a calf will behave when separated from its herd.

ACKNOWLEDGMENTS

Photographs: 6-7 Shona Wood, 8-9(b) Bob Langrish, 9(t) Kit Houghton, 10 Animal Photography/Sally-Anne Thompson, 11 Kit Houghton, 12 Animal Photography/Sally-Anne Thompson, 13 Syndication International, 14(t) Whitbread and Co Ltd, (b) Courage Shire Horse Centre, 15(t) Whitbread and Co Ltd, (b) Tony Stone Images, 17 Survival Anglia/Terry Andrewartha, 18-19 Bob Langrish, 20(t) Robert Harding Picture Library, (b) Explorer/François Gohier, 21 Robert Harding Picture Library, 22-3(t) Hutchison Library, (b) South American Pictures/Toni Morrison, 23(t) Hutchison Library, 24-5 David Simson/DAS Photos, 26 Animal Photography/R.Willbie, 27(tl) Okapia, (tr) Bildagentur Schuster/Waldkirch, (cl,cr,bl) David Simson/DAS Photos, (br) Zefa, 28-31 Eaglemoss/Nick Rains, 32-43 Eaglemoss/Shona Wood, 44-45 Eaglemoss/Nick Rains, 46-47 Eaglemoss/Shona Wood, 48-49 Tim Graham, 49 Britain on View, 50-51 Tim Graham, 52-54 Kit Houghton, 54-55 Tony Stone Images, 56-57 Mike Roberts, 58(t) Neil Holmes, (b) Mike Roberts, 59(t) Mike Roberts, (b) Tim Graham, 60, 61(t) Eaglemoss/Shona Wood, 61(c) Mike Roberts, (b) Tony Stone Images, 62 Bob Estall, 63-65 Eaglemoss/Shona Wood, 66-69 Eaglemoss/Steven Somerville, 70 Animal Photography/Vloo, 71-73 Bob Langrish, 74 Peter Roberts, 75-77 Frank Spooner Ltd/C.Vioujard, 78-79 Hutchison Library, 80 Eaglemoss/Elisabeth Weiland, 81 Zefa, 82(t) Eaglemoss/Elisabeth Weiland, (b) David Simson/DAS Photos, 83(t) Zefa, (b) Bruce Coleman Ltd/Fritz Prenzel, 84 Zefa, 85(tl,b) Nick Rains, (c) Zefa, 86-87 Nick Rains, 88-89 Zefa, 89 Dr. M. Beisert, 90(tl) Zefa/Elisabeth Weiland, (r) Explorer/Desjardins, 90-91 Dr. M. Beisert, 92-95 Hutchison Library, 96-97 Bruce Coleman Ltd/Henneghien, 97 Tony Stone Images, 98(t) Anne Bolt, (c) Explorer/M.Castéran, (b) Van Phillips, 99 AGE Fotostock, 100, 101(l) Frank Spooner Ltd/Marc Deville, 101(r) David Simson/DAS Photos, 102(tl,b) Frank Spooner Ltd/Marc Deville, 102-103(t) David Simson/DAS Photos, 103 Frank Spooner Ltd/Marc Deville, 104-107 Kit Houghton, 108-111 David Simson/DAS Photos, 112 Elisabeth Weiland, 113 Animal Photography/Sally-Anne Thompson, 114 Elisabeth Weiland, 115(t) Animal Photography/Sally-Anne Thompson, (c) Elisabeth Weiland, (b) Kit Houghton, 116-119 Elisabeth Weiland, 120-121 Shona Wood, 122-123 Bob Langrish, 124 The Slide File, (inset) Kit Houghton, 125(t) The Slide File, (b) Bob Langrish, 126-139 Eaglemoss/Shona Wood, 140(l,b) Eaglemoss/Shona Wood (r) Bob Langrish, 141-151 Eaglemoss/Shona Wood, 152-157 Bob Langrish, 158(t) Eaglemoss/Shona Wood, (b) Elisabeth Weiland, 159(t) Bruce Coleman Ltd/Fritz Prenzel, (c) Kit Houghton, (b) Elisabeth Weiland, 160-161 Kit Houghton, 162 Eaglemoss/Shona Wood, 162-163 Colorsport, 164 Tony Stone Images, 165 Eaglemoss/Shona Wood, 166 Allsport, 167, 168(t) Bob Langrish, 168(b) Colorsport, 169 Allsport, 170(l) Colorsport, (r) Bob Langrish, 171-173 Colorsport, 174 Elisabeth Weiland, 175 Karine Devilder, 176 Eaglemoss/Shona Wood, 176-177 Kit Houghton, 178-179 Elisabeth Weiland, 180(tl) Kit Houghton, (tr) Animal Photography/Sally-Anne Thompson, (b) Elisabeth Weiland, 181 Bob Langrish, 182 Karine Devilder, 183-191 Eaglemoss/Shona Wood.

Illustrations: 16-19 John Thompson/Garden Studios.